List of Contents

Introduction

In the vast expanse of our world, there exists a realm where dreams transcend the boundaries of reality, where financial freedom is not merely a distant wish, but a tangible destination. Welcome to the journey that awaits within the pages of "Making Your Own Money Machine." As we embark on this odyssey, we're not merely embarking on a quest for wealth, but rather, an expedition towards holistic abundance, purpose-driven existence, and the empowerment to sculpt your own financial destiny.

Imagine for a moment that your life is a canvas, waiting to be painted with the colors of your aspirations. Every stroke you make holds the potential to shape your financial landscape, and this book is your palette. It's a masterpiece that's been curated with years of experience, meticulous research, and the passion to propel you toward a brighter future. Let us cast aside the worn-out paradigms that confine our potential and embrace an ideology that thrives on creating, innovating, and seizing the opportunities that lie before us.

In the world of finance and business, the term "money machine" may conjure images of complicated algorithms and high-frequency trading. But as we traverse the chapters that follow, you'll come to understand that a money machine is not confined to the realm of software and systems—it resides within you. It's the amalgamation of your knowledge, your decisions, and your actions. It's about adopting the mindset of a wealth creator, of someone who sees beyond the immediate horizon and strives to establish a legacy that resonates through time.

As you delve into the chapters of this book, you'll be presented with a tapestry of insights that range from the art of passive income generation to the intricacies of ethical investing. The narrative is not a mere list of strategies; it's a symphony of knowledge and wisdom. Each chapter resonates with the harmonious rhythm of practical advice, real-world examples, and the guiding hand of a mentor who understands the nuances of the financial landscape.

But before we leap into the specifics, let's take a moment to reflect on the essence of financial success. It's not just about amassing wealth; it's about sculpting a life that's in alignment with your values, aspirations, and dreams. It's about nurturing your passions, embracing calculated risks, and navigating the labyrinth of opportunities that beckon at every turn. In essence, it's about creating a life that's enriched not only by monetary gains but also by the profound sense of fulfillment that accompanies the pursuit of purpose.

Consider this Introduction as the gateway to your journey. A journey where you'll unravel the secrets of making your money work for you, where you'll gain insights into the dynamic world of investments, and where you'll uncover the hidden gems of entrepreneurship. But remember, this journey is not meant to be a passive one. It's an invitation for you to engage actively, to introspect deeply, and to apply the knowledge you'll acquire to steer your life's course toward the horizon of your desires.

In the chapters that follow, you'll encounter the realm of passive income streams—a realm where your money is put to work even while you sleep. You'll discover the nuances of ethical investments, where your financial decisions resonate with your ethical compass. You'll delve into the world of entrepreneurship, where innovation, determination, and calculated risks converge to create transformative ventures.

Beyond the strategies, beyond the techniques, lies a philosophy that underscores every word you'll read. It's a philosophy that acknowledges the uniqueness of each journey, that respects the ebb and flow of market dynamics, and that recognizes the power of resilience in the face of challenges. This philosophy, dear reader, is what distinguishes a mere financial guide from a life-altering roadmap to success.

So, with your metaphorical boots laced and your figurative compass in hand, let us traverse the terrains of financial mastery. Let us navigate the labyrinth of opportunities with a steely resolve and a heart that's open to the infinite possibilities that await. The pages that follow are not just ink and paper; they're blueprints for action, guides for transformation, and keys to unlocking the doors that lead to your very own money machine—a machine that's powered by your knowledge, driven by your choices, and fueled by your dreams. The journey begins now, and the destination? It's limited only by your imagination.

Chapter 1: Understanding the Foundations of Wealth Creation

The Mindset of a Wealth Builder

In the world of financial success and wealth creation, the foundation is not just laid with monetary strategies and business acumen; it is deeply rooted in the mindset of the individual pursuing these aspirations. The journey towards building substantial wealth and attaining financial freedom begins with the right mental attitude – a mindset that is driven by growth, resilience, and a relentless pursuit of excellence.

Cultivating a Growth Mindset

At the core of every successful wealth builder is a growth mindset. This mindset, popularized by psychologist Carol Dweck, is the belief that abilities and intelligence can be developed through dedication, effort, and learning. A growth mindset opens the doors to endless possibilities, as it empowers individuals to embrace challenges and setbacks as opportunities for growth rather than indicators of failure. This mindset thrives on a willingness to continuously learn, adapt, and innovate.

Wealth builders with a growth mindset approach their endeavors with a sense of curiosity. They are not deterred by initial failures or setbacks; instead, they see them as stepping stones towards improvement. The growth mindset allows them to view obstacles as temporary hurdles that can be overcome through perseverance and strategic thinking. They understand that failures are not endpoints, but rather essential components of the journey that can lead to greater success.

Embracing Risk and Failure as Learning Opportunities
In the realm of wealth creation, risk is not just a buzzword; it's a stepping stone to achieving extraordinary results. Wealth builders who possess the right mindset do not shy away from calculated risks; they embrace them. They recognize that risk is an inherent aspect of any venture, and that avoiding it entirely often leads to missed opportunities for growth and reward.

Understanding that not every risk will yield the desired outcome, these individuals see failure as a valuable teacher. Each failure provides insights and lessons that can guide future decisions. The willingness to learn from mistakes is what sets apart those who thrive in the world of wealth creation from those who falter. Embracing failure as a learning opportunity also serves to reduce the fear of failure, allowing wealth builders to take bold actions and pursue ambitious goals.

Visualizing Success and Setting Clear Goals
A key aspect of the mindset of a wealth builder is the ability to envision success before it becomes a reality. Visualization is a powerful technique that involves creating a detailed mental image of your desired outcomes. By visualizing their goals, wealth builders create a roadmap for

their journey and foster a deep sense of motivation and determination.

However, visualization alone is not sufficient. Wealth builders couple it with the practice of setting clear and achievable goals. These goals serve as milestones along the path to success, breaking down the grand vision into actionable steps. They are specific, measurable, achievable, relevant, and time-bound (SMART). This clarity in goal-setting prevents vagueness and ensures that wealth builders are focused and purposeful in their actions.

Furthermore, the mindset of a wealth builder entails the commitment to regularly review and adjust goals as circumstances evolve. This adaptability ensures that the path to success remains aligned with changing opportunities and challenges. By constantly refining their objectives, wealth builders maintain a proactive stance and remain attuned to the dynamics of their journey.

The mindset of a wealth builder is a foundational pillar of the journey towards financial success and freedom. A growth mindset, the readiness to embrace risk and learn from failure, and the practice of visualizing success and setting clear goals collectively form the mental blueprint for realizing one's aspirations. This mindset propels individuals beyond conventional limitations and empowers them to navigate the complexities of wealth creation with resilience, determination, and unwavering focus.

Building a Strong Financial Foundation

In the dynamic world of finance and wealth creation, establishing a strong financial foundation is paramount. Just as a solid structure requires a stable base, your journey towards accumulating wealth and creating passive income streams starts with sound financial practices that lay the groundwork for your success. This subchapter delves into the critical components of building this strong financial foundation, emphasizing the significance of managing personal finances, creating an emergency fund, and effectively managing debt.

Managing Personal Finances and Budgeting

At the heart of your financial journey is the ability to manage personal finances effectively. This involves developing a comprehensive understanding of your income, expenses, and spending habits. Crafting and adhering to a well-structured budget is the cornerstone of this practice. A budget serves as a roadmap, allowing you to allocate resources consciously, curbing unnecessary expenditures while prioritizing savings and investments.

To construct a successful budget, start by categorizing your expenses into essential and discretionary categories. Essentials encompass necessities such as housing, utilities, groceries, and healthcare, while discretionary expenses include entertainment, dining out, and leisure activities. By tracking your spending over a few months, you can identify patterns and areas for potential savings.

The Importance of an Emergency Fund

Building a safety net in the form of an emergency fund is a
crucial component of financial preparedness. Life is replete
with unexpected events, from medical emergencies to job
losses or unexpected repairs. An emergency fund serves as
a buffer during these unforeseen circumstances, allowing
you to weather storms without derailing your financial
goals.

Financial experts recommend setting aside three to six
months' worth of living expenses in an easily accessible
account. This fund acts as a lifeline, providing peace of
mind and financial security. Having this safety net
minimizes the need to rely on high-interest debt or liquidate
investments during emergencies, safeguarding your long-
term financial health.

Reducing and Managing Debt Effectively

Debt can be a double-edged sword in the pursuit of wealth
creation. While it can serve as a tool for strategic
investments, such as education or real estate, excessive and
high-interest debt can impede your financial progress.
Prioritizing the reduction and management of debt is
pivotal for building a solid financial foundation.

Start by understanding the types of debt you carry.
Mortgage and student loan debts, for instance, often come
with manageable interest rates and potential tax benefits.
Conversely, credit card debt and high-interest personal
loans can accumulate rapidly and erode your financial
stability. Creating a repayment plan that focuses on paying

off high-interest debts first can help alleviate the burden and free up resources for savings and investments.

Building a robust financial foundation is the bedrock upon which your journey to wealth creation and passive income generation rests. By managing personal finances, adhering to a budget, establishing an emergency fund, and managing debt responsibly, you are equipping yourself with the essential tools needed to navigate the complex world of finance successfully. Remember, just as the tallest skyscrapers rise from solid foundations, your financial prosperity begins with these fundamental practices.

Navigating the World of Investments

Investing is the cornerstone of building wealth and achieving financial freedom. It's a journey that involves understanding various asset classes, assessing your risk tolerance, and developing strategies that align with your financial goals. In this sub chapter, we delve into the intricacies of navigating the world of investments, exploring the nuances of different asset classes, risk management, and the critical choice between short-term gains and long-term growth.

Differentiating between Asset Classes

When embarking on your investment journey, it's essential to comprehend the distinct characteristics of various asset classes. Each class represents a different opportunity for growth, with its own level of risk and return potential.

Stocks: Stocks represent ownership in a company and offer the potential for high returns. They are traded on stock exchanges, allowing investors to buy and sell shares. Investing in stocks provides the chance to participate in a company's success, but it also comes with volatility and risk.

Bonds: Bonds are debt instruments issued by governments or corporations to raise capital. When you invest in bonds, you're essentially lending money and receiving periodic interest payments. Bonds are generally considered less risky than stocks, making them an attractive option for conservative investors.

Real Estate: Real estate encompasses residential, commercial, and industrial properties. Real estate investments can offer rental income and the potential for property value appreciation. However, they also involve property management and market fluctuations.

Risk Tolerance and Diversification

Understanding your risk tolerance is a fundamental step in investment planning. Risk tolerance refers to your ability and willingness to handle the fluctuations in investment values. Factors such as age, financial goals, and personality play a role in determining your risk tolerance.

Diversification is a strategy that involves spreading your investments across different asset classes to reduce risk. By diversifying, you avoid putting all your eggs in one basket. If one asset class underperforms, the others may balance out the losses, thus minimizing overall risk.

Long-Term vs. Short-Term Investment Strategies
Investors often grapple with the decision of pursuing short-term gains or focusing on long-term growth. Each approach has its merits and considerations.

Long-Term Investments: Long-term investing involves holding onto assets for an extended period, typically several years or more. This strategy capitalizes on the power of compounding, where your investments generate returns that are reinvested over time. Long-term investing is associated with lower transaction costs and reduced impact from market fluctuations.

Short-Term Investments: Short-term investing aims to capitalize on immediate market fluctuations. It often involves more active management, as investors buy and sell assets within a shorter time frame. While short-term investments can yield quick profits, they also come with higher transaction costs and the potential for greater volatility.

In the world of investments, striking the right balance between short-term and long-term strategies requires careful consideration of your financial goals, risk tolerance, and investment horizon.

Navigating the world of investments is a crucial aspect of building wealth. By differentiating between asset classes, understanding your risk tolerance, and choosing the right investment horizon, you lay the groundwork for a successful investment journey. Remember, knowledge is your most potent tool – the more you educate yourself about investment options, the more confidently you can navigate the complexities of the financial markets.

Chapter 2: Generating Passive Income Streams

Leveraging the Power of Dividend Stocks

When it comes to generating passive income, few investment options offer the stability and potential for consistent returns quite like dividend stocks. In this subchapter, we will delve into the mechanics of dividend stocks, uncover their compelling benefits, explore the art of researching and selecting the right dividend-paying companies, and shed light on the smart strategy of reinvesting dividends to achieve compounded growth.

How Dividend Stocks Work and Their Benefits

Dividend stocks represent a unique facet of the stock market where companies share a portion of their earnings directly with shareholders. This distribution of profits is usually paid out in the form of dividends – cash payments or additional shares of stock. Companies that regularly issue dividends are often well-established, financially sound, and possess a history of steady revenue growth.

The allure of dividend stocks lies in their dual nature. Not only do they offer potential capital appreciation as stock prices rise over time, but they also provide a consistent stream of income. This makes them an attractive option for both income-seeking investors and those aiming for long-term growth. Dividend stocks can act as a stable anchor in an investment portfolio, cushioning against market volatility while delivering reliable returns.

Researching and Selecting Strong Dividend-Paying Companies

Identifying the right dividend-paying companies requires a careful blend of research, analysis, and understanding of various market dynamics. To start, look for companies with a history of consistent dividend payouts. A long track record of dividend payments indicates financial stability and management's commitment to shareholder value.

Financial metrics also play a vital role. A company's payout ratio – the proportion of earnings allocated to dividends – should be sustainable. A high payout ratio might raise concerns about the company's ability to invest in growth or withstand economic downturns. On the other hand, a low payout ratio might indicate a company is not sharing enough profits with shareholders.

Industry matters too. Industries with stable demand and predictable revenue tend to be more reliable dividend sources. Additionally, consider the company's growth potential. A company that not only offers dividends but also reinvests in itself to expand can be a strong contender for your investment dollars.

Reinvesting Dividends for Compounded Growth

The power of compounding is a force to be reckoned with in the world of finance, and dividend stocks provide a perfect vehicle for leveraging this power. When you reinvest dividends – instead of pocketing them – you purchase additional shares of the same stock. Over time, these additional shares accumulate and generate more dividends of their own. This cycle repeats, leading to exponential growth over the long term.

Imagine owning shares of a dividend-paying company for several years. The dividends you receive aren't just passive income; they're also opportunities for your investment to grow. As you reinvest those dividends, your ownership stake in the company increases, which in turn leads to more dividends in the future. This self-reinforcing cycle results in a snowball effect, where your investment gradually gains momentum and multiplies.

Reinvesting dividends offers a disciplined way to achieve compounded growth without the need for continuous manual adjustments to your investment portfolio. This strategy is particularly powerful when employed over extended periods, allowing your money to work harder for you.

Dividend stocks are a remarkable tool for generating passive income and building wealth over time. They provide the dual benefit of potential capital appreciation and consistent income, making them an attractive choice for investors seeking both stability and growth. By thoroughly researching and selecting strong dividend-paying companies and strategically reinvesting dividends, investors can harness the power of compounding to create a formidable income-generating machine that steadily advances toward their financial goals.

Real Estate Ventures for Passive Income

In the realm of generating passive income streams, few avenues are as time-tested and potentially lucrative as real estate investments. The allure of real estate lies not only in the potential for consistent cash flow but also in the ability to build substantial wealth over time. This sub chapter delves into the intricate world of real estate ventures for passive income, guiding you through the key steps and considerations to embark on this journey.

Exploring Rental Properties and Real Estate Investment Trusts (REITs)

When it comes to generating passive income through real estate, rental properties and Real Estate Investment Trusts (REITs) stand out as prominent avenues. Rental properties involve purchasing residential or commercial real estate with the intention of leasing it out to tenants. This can provide a consistent stream of rental income, which, when managed effectively, can create a reliable source of passive earnings.

On the other hand, REITs offer a more accessible approach to real estate investment. A REIT is a company that owns or finances income-producing real estate in various sectors, such as apartments, office buildings, retail centers, or even hotels. Investing in REITs allows you to indirectly invest in real estate without the responsibilities of property management. The dividends paid out by REITs can constitute a significant portion of your passive income portfolio.

Property Selection, Financing, and Property Management

Selecting the right properties is a cornerstone of successful real estate investment. Thorough market research and due diligence are essential to identify properties with strong income potential and the likelihood for property value appreciation. Factors such as location, demographics, market trends, and local amenities should be meticulously analyzed to make informed decisions.

Financing plays a crucial role in real estate ventures. Investors often use a combination of personal funds and loans to acquire properties. Mortgages, hard money loans, and creative financing methods are common approaches. Calculating the Return on Investment (ROI) is crucial, factoring in expenses such as mortgage payments, property taxes, insurance, maintenance, and potential vacancies.

Effective property management is key to maintaining a steady stream of income. This involves tenant screening, lease agreements, rent collection, and property maintenance. Whether you choose to manage properties yourself or hire a property management company, ensuring a positive tenant experience and the upkeep of the property are paramount for sustained profitability.

Mitigating Risks and Maximizing Returns in Real Estate

While the potential for passive income in real estate is promising, it's not without risks. Market fluctuations, property damage, unforeseen expenses, and economic downturns are all potential challenges. Mitigating these risks requires a combination of preparation, knowledge, and a well-structured investment strategy.

Diversification is a powerful risk management tool. Spreading your investments across different types of properties and locations can help reduce the impact of localized market fluctuations. Moreover, staying informed about local and national real estate trends allows you to make educated decisions and adjust your strategy accordingly.

To maximize returns, consider value-add strategies. These involve making strategic improvements to the property to enhance its value and increase rental income. Renovations, upgrades, and improved property management practices can attract higher-quality tenants willing to pay premium rents.

Real estate ventures hold significant potential for creating passive income streams. Whether through rental properties or REITs, the right investment decisions, effective management, and risk mitigation strategies are pivotal for long-term success. By understanding the nuances of property selection, financing, management, and risk management, you can harness the power of real estate to create a steady flow of passive income while building tangible wealth over time. Remember, real estate investing requires commitment, continuous learning, and a patient approach, but the rewards can be substantial for those who navigate the path wisely.

Creating and Selling Digital Products

In the rapidly evolving landscape of business and finance, one avenue that has gained significant traction for generating passive income is the creation and sale of digital products. With the advent of the internet and technological advancements, individuals have unprecedented opportunities to monetize their expertise, creativity, and knowledge by packaging them into valuable digital products. Whether you're an entrepreneur, a freelancer, or someone looking to diversify income streams, this sub chapter delves into the intricate process of creating, marketing, and profiting from digital products.

Identifying Your Niche and Audience

At the heart of any successful digital product venture lies a deep understanding of your target niche and audience. Niche selection is critical, as it helps you cater to a specific group of people who share common interests or pain points. Research is your ally here – delve into market trends, identify gaps, and uncover problems your audience is seeking solutions for. By niching down, you not only differentiate yourself but also establish credibility within your chosen domain.

Next, comprehending your audience's needs and preferences is paramount. Conduct surveys, engage in discussions on relevant online platforms, and gather insights into what challenges they're facing. By addressing their pain points, you're positioning yourself as a problem solver, fostering trust and connection.

Developing Valuable Digital Products

Once you've identified your niche and understood your audience's requirements, it's time to translate your expertise into compelling digital products. These products can span a diverse range, including ebooks, online courses, webinars, templates, software, and more. Here's a closer look at each:

- **Ebooks**: Ebooks are an excellent way to share in-depth knowledge. They can be guides, manuals, or even comprehensive resources on a particular subject.

- **Online Courses**: Offering online courses allows you to impart skills and knowledge systematically. The format could include video lectures, quizzes, assignments, and certificates upon completion.

- **Webinars**: Hosting webinars enables real-time interaction with your audience. These can be one-off sessions or part of a series, covering topics of interest.

- **Templates and Tools**: Creating templates, spreadsheets, or software tools tailored to your audience's needs can be incredibly valuable. These save time and effort for users while generating passive income for you.

Setting Up Sales Funnels and Marketing Strategies

Building exceptional digital products is just one piece of the puzzle; effectively marketing and selling them is equally crucial. Enter the concept of sales funnels. A sales funnel is a strategic process that guides potential customers from awareness to making a purchase. Here's a simplified breakdown:

1. Awareness: Attract your audience's attention through content marketing, social media, and other online channels.

2. Interest: Engage your audience with compelling content, offering them valuable insights and information related to your digital product's subject matter.

3. Consideration: Present your digital product as the solution to their pain points. This could involve testimonials, case studies, and more in-depth information about what your product offers.

4. Conversion: This is the ultimate goal – getting your audience to make a purchase. This step can be facilitated through discounts, limited-time offers, or special bonuses.

5. Retention: After the sale, maintain a connection with your customers. Provide value through additional resources, exclusive content, and updates about related products.

Effective marketing strategies are diverse, from leveraging social media platforms to email marketing campaigns. Consistency and authenticity are key – your marketing efforts should reflect your expertise and resonate with your audience's needs.

The world of generating passive income through digital products offers a remarkable avenue for individuals with expertise, knowledge, and creativity. By identifying your niche and audience, developing valuable digital products, and implementing well-structured sales funnels and marketing strategies, you can create a sustainable source of income while adding value to your customers' lives. The digital realm presents opportunities limited only by your imagination and dedication, making it an exciting frontier for those seeking financial success and entrepreneurial growth.

Chapter 3: Entrepreneurship and Business Ventures

Launching a Profitable Startup

In the realm of entrepreneurship, launching a startup that thrives in today's competitive landscape requires more than just a brilliant idea; it necessitates a well-thought-out strategy, meticulous planning, and a relentless pursuit of excellence. This sub chapter delves into the intricate process of turning innovative ideas into successful businesses, starting from the initial spark of creativity to securing funding and propelling sustainable growth.

Identifying Market Gaps and Innovative Ideas

In the grand tapestry of business success, the thread that often binds prosperous startups together is a keen eye for identifying market gaps and addressing them with innovative solutions. The process begins with an in-depth analysis of industry trends, consumer behavior, and pain points that have yet to be effectively addressed. By scrutinizing these spaces, entrepreneurs position themselves to create products or services that are not only relevant but also capable of disrupting the status quo.

Innovation is the beating heart of entrepreneurship. It drives entrepreneurs to explore new technologies, challenge traditional business models, and reimagine processes. Beyond that, it involves understanding the shifting needs and preferences of consumers and predicting the future direction of industries. It's about finding novel ways to solve age-old problems and bringing fresh perspectives to age-old markets.

Crafting a Solid Business Plan and Securing Funding
An innovative idea alone, however brilliant, is insufficient to guide a startup to success. A well-structured business plan serves as the roadmap that outlines every facet of the venture's journey. This blueprint includes a detailed analysis of the target market, a clear value proposition, a competitive analysis, and a comprehensive marketing strategy. It lays out the financial projections, highlighting revenue streams and anticipated expenses, while providing a strategic framework for achieving growth milestones.

With a robust business plan in hand, the next critical step is securing funding. Financing is the lifeblood of startups, fueling their growth and development. Entrepreneurs have a variety of funding options, ranging from bootstrapping and angel investors to venture capital and crowdfunding. Each avenue has its merits and challenges, and the choice often depends on the stage of the startup, the industry, and the entrepreneur's vision.

Investors are not merely looking for a great idea; they seek a viable business model, a dedicated team, and a clear path to profitability. Crafting a compelling pitch that showcases these elements is essential for attracting funding. Entrepreneurs need to demonstrate a deep understanding of their market, their competitors, and their unique value proposition. By communicating the potential for growth and return on investment, entrepreneurs can inspire confidence in potential backers.

Scaling and Sustaining the Startup's Growth
Launching a startup is just the first step in a long and challenging journey. Once the venture gains traction and achieves initial success, entrepreneurs must focus on scaling their operations to reach a broader audience. This phase requires efficient processes, effective team management, and the ability to maintain quality even as the business expands.

Entrepreneurs must be prepared to iterate on their business model and adapt to changing circumstances. As a startup grows, it will encounter new challenges and opportunities that demand flexibility and innovation. Scaling doesn't just involve expanding the customer base; it also involves managing increased demand, optimizing supply chains, and maintaining a strong company culture.

Sustaining growth over the long term requires a relentless commitment to continuous improvement. Entrepreneurs must be vigilant about staying attuned to market shifts, gathering customer feedback, and evolving their offerings to meet evolving needs. This adaptability ensures that a startup remains relevant and competitive even as the business landscape evolves.

Launching a profitable startup is an exhilarating yet demanding endeavor. The process starts with identifying market gaps and innovative ideas, guided by a commitment to solving real-world problems. Crafting a solid business plan and securing funding are essential steps that lay the foundation for growth. Finally, scaling and sustaining a startup's growth requires a combination of strategic thinking, adaptability, and an unwavering dedication to delivering value to customers. The journey is marked by challenges and triumphs, and entrepreneurs who navigate it with resilience and determination have the potential to create transformative businesses that leave an indelible mark on the world.

E-commerce and Dropshipping Strategies

E-commerce has revolutionized the way business is conducted, providing entrepreneurs with unprecedented opportunities to reach a global audience and establish thriving enterprises from the comfort of their own spaces. Within the vast landscape of e-commerce, the dropshipping model stands out as an increasingly popular approach, offering a low-risk entry point for aspiring business owners. In this sub chapter, we delve into the intricacies of e-commerce and explore the strategies behind successful dropshipping ventures.

Understanding the E-commerce Landscape

E-commerce, short for electronic commerce, refers to the buying and selling of goods and services over the internet.

Its allure lies in its accessibility and the ability to reach customers across geographical boundaries. A critical advantage of e-commerce is the elimination of the traditional brick-and-mortar store's physical limitations, enabling businesses to tap into a global market.

Dropshipping Business

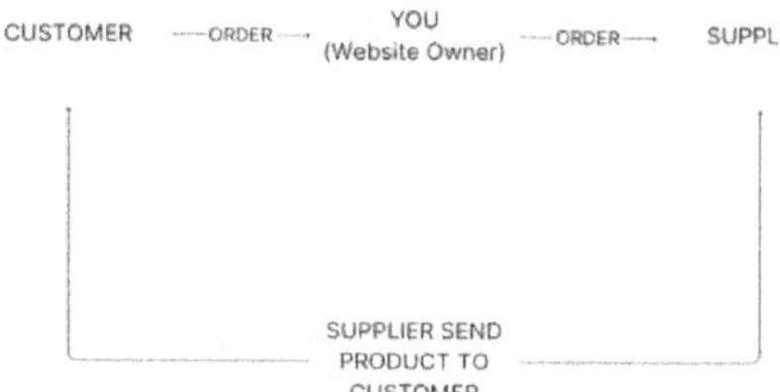

Within the e-commerce realm, various business models exist, ranging from direct sales to subscription services. One standout model, dropshipping, has gained substantial traction due to its low barriers to entry. Dropshipping involves a simplified supply chain, where the retailer doesn't hold physical inventory. Instead, when a customer places an order, the retailer purchases the item from a third-party supplier who then ships the product directly to the customer. This approach minimizes upfront costs and inventory management complexities.

Selecting Products, Suppliers, and Platforms
One of the cornerstones of a successful dropshipping venture is selecting the right products to offer. This

decision hinges on thorough market research and an understanding of consumer demand. Identifying a niche that resonates with your target audience and offers products with a balance of demand and profitability is key. The process involves delving into market trends, competitor analysis, and customer preferences.

Equally vital is establishing partnerships with reliable suppliers. The quality of your supplier's products, shipping times, and customer service can significantly impact your business's reputation. Dedicating time to vetting potential suppliers and cultivating strong relationships with them ensures smoother operations and customer satisfaction. Platforms like Alibaba, Oberlo, and SaleHoo can serve as valuable resources for finding reputable suppliers.

Building a Strong Online Presence and Customer Base
In the digital age, a strong online presence is non-negotiable for e-commerce success. Building an engaging and user-friendly online store is the foundation. Choose an e-commerce platform that aligns with your needs, whether it's Shopify, WooCommerce, or others. These platforms offer customizable templates and integrations that streamline the purchasing process.

A robust digital marketing strategy is the driving force behind attracting and retaining customers. Utilize search engine optimization (SEO) techniques to improve your store's visibility on search engines. Leverage social media platforms to showcase your products, engage with your audience, and build a loyal community. Email marketing campaigns can nurture leads and encourage repeat business.

Customer experience should be at the forefront of your efforts. Provide clear product descriptions, high-quality images, and transparent pricing. Streamline the checkout process to reduce cart abandonment. Implement effective customer support channels to address inquiries promptly and resolve issues, fostering trust and loyalty.

E-commerce, particularly through the dropshipping model, opens doors for aspiring entrepreneurs to enter the business world with reduced risks and costs. Understanding the e-commerce landscape, selecting the right products and suppliers, and building a compelling online presence are pivotal steps in creating a flourishing dropshipping venture. As you embark on this journey, remember that success requires continuous adaptation, innovation, and a dedication to delivering exceptional value to your customers. The world of e-commerce is ever-evolving, and by staying informed and employing effective strategies, you can carve your path to entrepreneurial success.

Franchising and Licensing for Passive Income

Franchising and licensing have emerged as powerful strategies for individuals seeking passive income streams and business ownership without necessarily starting a venture from scratch. These approaches allow aspiring entrepreneurs to leverage established brands, business models, and systems, while minimizing the challenges typically associated with building a business from the ground up. In this sub chapter, we will delve into the world of franchising and licensing, exploring the opportunities they present, how to evaluate them, and the key considerations for managing and expanding these ventures.

Exploring Franchising and Licensing Opportunities
Franchising and licensing are business models that grant individuals the right to operate a business under an established brand's name and guidelines. These models provide a win-win situation for both parties involved – the franchisor (or licensor) and the franchisee (or licensee). Franchisors offer their proven business concepts, products, and support in exchange for franchise fees and a percentage of the profits.

Licensing, on the other hand, involves granting permission to others to use intellectual property such as trademarks, patents, or copyrights. This can span a wide range of industries, from technology and entertainment to consumer goods and services.

For individuals seeking passive income, franchising and licensing offer several advantages. They provide a ready-made business model with a track record of success, established branding, and ongoing support. Franchisees and licensees benefit from access to training, marketing materials, and a network of fellow business owners.

Evaluating Franchise Options and Legal Considerations
Selecting the right franchise or licensing opportunity is critical for long-term success. The first step is conducting thorough research. Investigate the franchise's history, financial performance, and reputation within the industry. Seek out feedback from current and past franchisees to gain insights into the business's actual operations and support system.

Legal considerations play a significant role in franchising and licensing. Franchise agreements and licensing contracts are legally binding documents that outline the terms of the relationship, including fees, territory rights, intellectual property usage, and operational guidelines. It's imperative to have legal counsel review these documents to ensure you fully understand your rights and responsibilities.

Managing and Expanding Your Franchised Business
Once you've entered the world of franchising or licensing, effectively managing and expanding your business becomes the next priority. One of the advantages of these models is the existing support structure provided by the franchisor or licensor. Regular communication, training programs, and updates on industry trends are typically offered to help you stay competitive.

Expansion within the franchised model involves opening additional locations or outlets, often within the same territory. This allows you to tap into economies of scale and increase your reach. However, expansion should be carefully planned to maintain quality control and consistency across all locations.

Franchising and licensing present exciting opportunities for individuals seeking to generate passive income and become business owners without the complexities of starting from scratch. By exploring these models, evaluating options thoroughly, and managing your franchise or license effectively, you can build a profitable and scalable business venture. Remember, while the path to success in franchising and licensing may be guided by established systems, your dedication, commitment, and careful decision-making remain pivotal to achieving your financial goals and entrepreneurial dreams.

Chapter 4: Mastering the Art of Personal Branding

The Importance of Personal Branding

In an era characterized by rapid technological advancement and interconnectedness, personal branding has emerged as a pivotal tool in the world of business and finance. It's not just about marketing yourself; it's about crafting a distinct identity that resonates with your target audience. In this subchapter, we delve into the profound significance of personal branding, exploring how it involves defining your unique value proposition, building an authentic online presence, and establishing credibility and trust within your industry.

Defining Your Unique Value Proposition

Your unique value proposition (UVP) is the cornerstone of your personal brand. It encapsulates the essence of what you bring to the table that sets you apart from the competition. Your UVP is a combination of your skills, experiences, expertise, and the unique perspectives you offer. To define your UVP, consider the following:

1. Self-Reflection: Take a deep dive into your strengths, passions, and areas of expertise. What problems can you solve? What solutions can you provide? Align these qualities with the needs of your target audience.

2. Market Research: Analyze your industry and identify gaps or areas that need innovation. How can your UVP address these gaps? Research your competitors to understand their branding strategies and identify opportunities for differentiation.

3. Clarity: Your UVP should be succinct and clear. It's the promise you make to your audience about what they can expect from you. Craft a compelling statement that communicates your value succinctly.

Building an Authentic Online Presence
In today's digital age, your online presence is often the first impression you make on potential clients, partners, and employers. Building an authentic online presence goes beyond flashy graphics; it's about showcasing your personality, values, and expertise in a genuine manner:

1. Consistent Branding: Use consistent branding elements such as colors, fonts, and a professional headshot across all your online profiles. This creates a cohesive and memorable visual identity.

2. Engaging Content: Share valuable content that demonstrates your expertise and offers insights to your audience. This could be through blog posts, videos, podcasts, or social media updates. Engaging content establishes you as a thought leader and builds trust.

3. Interactivity: Interact with your audience by responding to comments, engaging in conversations, and participating in online communities. This shows that you're approachable and genuinely interested in connecting.

Establishing Credibility and Trust Within Your Industry
Credibility and trust are the bedrock of any successful personal brand. Building and maintaining them require a strategic approach:

1. Expertise: Continuously invest in your professional development to deepen your expertise. Attend industry conferences, take courses, and stay up-to-date with the latest trends and advancements.

2. Testimonials and Case Studies: Share success stories and testimonials from satisfied clients or customers. These real-life examples demonstrate your ability to deliver results.

3. Networking and Collaborations: Forge connections with other experts in your field. Collaborating with respected individuals or organizations can lend credibility to your personal brand.

4. Transparency: Be open about your journey, including successes and failures. Sharing your experiences humanizes you and makes your brand more relatable.

Personal branding is not a mere vanity exercise; it's a strategic approach to carving a distinctive identity in a competitive landscape. Your unique value proposition, authentic online presence, and credibility are the pillars that uphold your personal brand. When done right, personal branding has the potential to unlock opportunities, attract the right audience, and position you as a trusted authority in your industry. In the chapters to come, we will delve deeper into actionable strategies for crafting and enhancing your personal brand to propel your journey towards financial success and business growth.

Leveraging Social Media for Business Growth

In today's interconnected digital landscape, the role of social media in shaping businesses and personal brands cannot be overstated. In this sub-chapter, we will explore the profound impact that social media platforms can have on business growth and the strategies that can be employed to harness this potential to the fullest extent.

Choosing the Right Social Media Platforms

Before embarking on your social media journey, it's essential to discern which platforms align with your business objectives and target audience. Each platform has its distinct user base, tone, and content format, making a tailored approach necessary for success.

- **Facebook**: With its massive user base and diverse demographics, Facebook offers a versatile space for businesses to engage with a wide range of potential customers. It accommodates various content formats, including text posts, images, videos, and live streams, enabling businesses to experiment with different forms of engagement.

- **Instagram**: This platform thrives on visual storytelling and is a haven for businesses with visually appealing products or services. Its emphasis on aesthetics demands a carefully curated feed that resonates with your brand identity. Instagram's Stories feature provides an excellent opportunity for real-time updates, behind-the-scenes glimpses, and short-lived promotions.

- **LinkedIn**: Ideal for B2B networking and professional brand building, LinkedIn is a platform where thought leadership and industry expertise are highly valued. Sharing informative articles, industry insights, and connecting with peers and potential clients can significantly elevate your brand's reputation.

- **Twitter**: Known for its brevity, Twitter is a dynamic platform for sharing timely updates, participating in trending conversations, and demonstrating thought leadership within your niche. Its fast-paced nature requires frequent engagement to maintain visibility and relevance.

- **YouTube**: If your brand can leverage video content effectively, YouTube offers a platform for in-depth tutorials, behind-the-scenes content, and product demonstrations. Videos have the power to engage and educate your audience in a format that often feels more personal and informative.

Creating Engaging Content and Fostering Community
Engaging content is the lifeblood of social media success. To make an impact, it's crucial to understand your target

audience's preferences, pain points, and aspirations. Authenticity is the cornerstone of building a strong brand presence.

- **Storytelling**: Sharing compelling narratives about your brand's journey, challenges, and triumphs humanizes your business and builds emotional connections with your audience. Stories have the power to create empathy and relatability.

- **Visual Appeal**: High-quality visuals are a non-negotiable aspect of social media. Eye-catching images, well-designed graphics, and professionally produced videos command attention in users' fast-scrolling feeds.

- **User-Generated Content**: Encouraging your customers to share their experiences with your products or services creates a sense of community and authenticity. When potential customers see positive experiences from real people, it fosters trust and credibility.

- **Consistency**: Consistent posting maintains your brand's visibility and keeps your audience engaged. Develop a content calendar that outlines when and what you'll post. This also helps you plan ahead for special events, promotions, or launches.

Fostering a community goes beyond one-way communication. Responding to comments, acknowledging user-generated content, and actively engaging with your audience demonstrates that you value their input and are genuinely interested in building a relationship.

Converting Followers into Customers and Clients
While engagement and community-building are crucial, the ultimate goal is to translate this engagement into tangible business outcomes. Converting social media followers into loyal customers requires strategic planning and a customer-centric approach.

- **Effective Call to Action (CTA):** Every post should guide your audience on the next step to take. Whether it's visiting your website, subscribing to your newsletter, or making a purchase, a clear and compelling CTA is essential.

- **Delivering Value**: Consistently provide value to your audience. Share insightful content, exclusive offers, or educational resources that cater to their needs. When followers see the benefits of engaging with your brand, they're more likely to become customers.

- **Utilizing Analytics**: Social media platforms provide robust analytics that reveal the performance of your posts. Monitoring engagement metrics, click-through rates, and conversion rates helps you understand what's working and what needs improvement.

- **Optimized Landing Pages**: When directing followers to your website, ensure that the landing page is relevant to the content they engaged with. A seamless transition from social media to your website enhances the user experience and increases the chances of conversion.

The potential of social media as a powerful tool for business growth cannot be underestimated. By carefully selecting the right platforms, creating engaging content, fostering a sense of community, and strategically converting followers into customers, businesses can not only amplify their brand presence but also build meaningful relationships with their audience. A successful social media strategy is an art that blends creativity, data-driven decision-making, and a deep understanding of human psychology to create a dynamic and impactful brand narrative.

Networking and Building Strategic Relationships

In the ever-evolving landscape of business and entrepreneurship, mastering the art of personal branding has become paramount. It's no longer enough to simply provide a product or service; your personal brand is the bridge that connects you with your audience, builds trust, and fosters lasting relationships. Within this chapter, we delve into the critical importance of networking and strategic relationship-building, two cornerstones of personal branding that can propel your success to unprecedented heights.

The Power of Networking in Business Success

Networking, often cited as a clichéd buzzword, is an intricate web of connections and interactions that has the potential to be the catalyst for immense growth. In an interconnected world, the value of cultivating a robust network cannot be overstated. Networking is not solely about attending events and exchanging business cards; it's about creating authentic, meaningful relationships that transcend the superficial.

Effective networking can open doors to opportunities you might never have imagined. It's not just about what you know; it's about who you know and, more importantly, who knows you. By strategically positioning yourself in relevant circles, you increase your chances of coming across potential clients, collaborators, and mentors.

A successful networking approach involves active listening, genuine interest in others, and an understanding of the value you can offer. While digital platforms have expanded our reach, face-to-face interactions still hold unparalleled power. Conferences, workshops, and seminars provide arenas to not only learn but also to connect on a personal level. Remember, your network is not built overnight; it's cultivated through consistent effort, authenticity, and a willingness to give as much as you receive.

Nurturing Relationships for Mutual Growth
Networking is merely the initial step; the real magic happens when you transition from casual acquaintances to trusted allies. Nurturing relationships is about investing time and effort into maintaining connections and demonstrating your commitment to mutual success. This involves regular communication, sharing valuable insights, and showing support for your connections' endeavors.

When nurturing relationships, quality triumphs over quantity. It's better to have a small circle of genuinely supportive connections than a large network with no meaningful interactions. By fostering trust and rapport, you position yourself as a valuable resource—a person others turn to when seeking advice, collaboration, or partnership.

Collaborations, Partnerships, and Joint Ventures
In the realm of business, partnerships and collaborations have the potential to exponentially amplify your reach and impact. When aligned with the right individuals or organizations, these ventures can lead to the creation of something far greater than what you could achieve alone.

Collaborations take various forms, ranging from joint marketing campaigns to co-developing products or services. The key is to find partners whose strengths complement yours, allowing for a harmonious synergy. A successful partnership isn't just about combining resources; it's about shared values, mutual goals, and a clear understanding of each other's roles and contributions.

Strategic relationships extend beyond one-time collaborations. Long-term partnerships often involve formal agreements and shared responsibilities, such as joint ventures. These ventures involve pooling resources, expertise, and risks to achieve common objectives. Joint ventures can lead to diversified revenue streams, expanded customer bases, and the opportunity to tap into markets that might otherwise be inaccessible.

Networking and building strategic relationships are integral components of personal branding that propel you beyond the realm of transactions into the realm of transformational interactions. As you master the art of personal branding, remember that relationships are the currency of business, and the effort you invest in nurturing them can yield returns that are not only financial but also deeply rewarding on a personal level. In an interconnected world, success is no longer a solo journey; it's a collaborative symphony that resonates with the power of partnerships and the strength of genuine connections.

Chapter 5: Exploring Innovative Investment Opportunities

Cryptocurrencies and Blockchain Investments

Cryptocurrencies and the underlying technology of blockchain have revolutionized the financial landscape, offering individuals and investors unprecedented opportunities for growth and diversification. In this subchapter, we'll delve into the intricacies of blockchain technology, explore various types of cryptocurrencies, and provide a comprehensive understanding of the risks and rewards associated with investing in this dynamic space.

Understanding Blockchain Technology

At the heart of the cryptocurrency phenomenon lies blockchain technology—a decentralized and secure digital ledger that records transactions across multiple computers. Blockchain's defining feature is its immutability, meaning that once a transaction is recorded, it cannot be altered without consensus from the network. This transparency and security have immense implications, not only for cryptocurrencies but also for various industries such as supply chain management, healthcare, and more.

Blockchain technology operates through a network of nodes, each validating and recording transactions through complex cryptographic algorithms. This eliminates the need for intermediaries like banks, reducing transaction costs and enhancing efficiency. The technology's potential extends far beyond cryptocurrencies, shaping the future of data management and security.

Assessing Different Types of Cryptocurrencies

Cryptocurrencies represent a diverse array of digital assets, each with its own unique characteristics and use cases. The pioneering cryptocurrency, Bitcoin, is often considered digital gold and a store of value due to its limited supply and deflationary nature. Ethereum, on the other hand, introduced smart contracts and decentralized applications, enabling the creation of various projects on its platform.

Beyond Bitcoin and Ethereum, there are thousands of altcoins, each catering to specific purposes. Ripple (XRP) focuses on facilitating cross-border payments, while Litecoin (LTC) boasts faster transaction times. Binance Coin (BNB) powers the Binance exchange and offers utility within its ecosystem. The diversity of cryptocurrencies allows investors to diversify their portfolios based on their risk tolerance and investment goals.

Managing the Risks and Rewards of Crypto Investments

While cryptocurrencies offer compelling opportunities, they also come with inherent risks that must be understood and managed. The volatility of cryptocurrency prices is a defining characteristic of the market. Prices can experience significant fluctuations within short periods, leading to both substantial gains and losses. Investors need to be prepared for this high level of volatility and should only invest what they can afford to lose.

Security is another critical consideration in the cryptocurrency space. While blockchain technology is inherently secure, external factors such as exchange hacks and scams can compromise investments. Storing cryptocurrencies in secure wallets, including hardware wallets and cold storage solutions, is imperative to protect assets from potential breaches.

To navigate the risks and maximize rewards, thorough research is essential. This includes understanding the technology, the team behind the project, the use case, and the broader market trends. Diversification is also a key strategy to mitigate risk. By spreading investments across different cryptocurrencies and assets, investors can reduce the impact of a single asset's poor performance.

The world of cryptocurrencies and blockchain investments presents both exciting opportunities and challenges. Understanding the technology's fundamentals, assessing the various types of cryptocurrencies available, and managing the risks associated with the market's volatility are essential steps for any investor looking to participate in this innovative space. As with any investment, due diligence, education, and a long-term perspective are the cornerstones of successful cryptocurrency investing.

Peer-to-Peer Lending and Crowdfunding

In the ever-evolving realm of modern finance, where innovation is the cornerstone of growth, new avenues for investment have emerged, reshaping the traditional landscape. Peer-to-Peer (P2P) lending and crowdfunding stand at the forefront of these innovations, democratizing the investment sphere and offering individuals unique ways to diversify their portfolios while seeking potentially higher returns. This sub chapter delves deep into the intricate mechanics, benefits, and vital considerations associated with P2P lending and crowdfunding.

Exploring P2P Lending Platforms

Peer-to-Peer lending platforms represent a significant departure from the conventional lending ecosystem. These platforms serve as intermediaries, connecting borrowers – often individuals, small businesses, or startups – with individual lenders looking to invest their funds. This direct connection bypasses the need for traditional financial institutions, fostering a more efficient and inclusive lending environment.

The benefits of P2P lending extend to both borrowers and lenders. Borrowers can access funds quickly, often with more flexible terms than traditional bank loans, making it an appealing alternative for those who may not meet stringent bank requirements. On the lender's side, P2P lending offers a way to earn interest on their capital, potentially yielding higher returns compared to the interest earned on savings accounts or bonds.

P2P lending platforms typically categorize loans based on risk profiles, and investors can select loans that align with their risk tolerance. These platforms often provide information about the borrowers, the purpose of the loan, and the interest rate. While the potential for attractive returns exists, it's imperative to recognize that the higher returns often correspond to higher risks, especially for loans with lower creditworthiness.

Investing in Startups through Crowdfunding
Crowdfunding has experienced a meteoric rise, transforming the way startups and creative ventures secure funding. Crowdfunding platforms serve as virtual stages where entrepreneurs showcase their projects to a global audience, inviting them to contribute funds in exchange for rewards, products, or even equity.

The significance of crowdfunding transcends mere capital infusion. It serves as a litmus test for market demand. A successfully funded campaign provides a direct channel to validate concepts and gauge interest before committing extensive resources. For investors, crowdfunding platforms unlock opportunities to invest in early-stage companies, aligning investments with personal passions and interests.

Crowdfunding manifests in several models: reward-based, donation-based, debt-based, and equity-based. Equity based crowdfunding allows investors to acquire a stake in the company, potentially resulting in substantial returns if the venture succeeds.

Evaluating Potential Risks and Returns
While P2P lending and crowdfunding offer tantalizing prospects, a prudent investor must meticulously assess the associated risks and rewards.

P2P Lending: Risks and Rewards

The foremost risk in P2P lending is the borrower's default. Economic fluctuations and unforeseen circumstances can impact a borrower's ability to repay. However, platforms employ credit-scoring mechanisms to evaluate borrowers' creditworthiness, providing a degree of risk mitigation. Diversification, spreading investments across multiple loans, can further mitigate risk.

The rewards in P2P lending manifest as interest income. The interest rates vary based on loan risk and the platform itself. It's vital to scrutinize platforms diligently, considering historical returns, transparency, and available diversification tools.

Crowdfunding: Risks and Rewards

The central risk in crowdfunding centers on project or startup success. Not all ventures will achieve their goals, and not all products will resonate with consumers. As an investor, careful scrutiny of project details, business plans, and the background of creators is essential.

On the flip side, the rewards can be substantial. Equity-based crowdfunding, in particular, offers the prospect of capitalizing on early-stage successes. However, it's crucial to acknowledge that investing in startups inherently involves risk, and the journey from idea to profitability can be tumultuous.

Peer-to-Peer lending and crowdfunding epitomize the democratization of finance, empowering individuals to engage with investment strategies previously reserved for institutions. These innovative models introduce new dynamics to investment portfolios, providing diversification and potential high returns. Yet, they necessitate thorough research, disciplined due diligence, and a clear understanding of personal risk tolerance.

In navigating the intricacies of P2P lending and crowdfunding, vigilance reigns supreme. Proper risk management, meticulous selection of opportunities, and a strategic approach to diversification are the cornerstones of success. As with any investment venture, knowledge is your ultimate weapon. Embrace the dynamic and transformative potential of these methods with prudence and confidence.

The Future of Investing: AI and Automation

In the realm of investment strategies, few developments have sparked as much excitement and transformation as the integration of artificial intelligence (AI) and automation. This merging of cutting-edge technology with traditional investment practices has given rise to a new era in finance—one that is reshaping the landscape of wealth creation and management. In this subchapter, we will delve into the intricate world of AI-driven investment strategies, exploring the ways in which AI is revolutionizing the industry, the role of robo-advisors and algorithmic trading, and the delicate balance between automation and human decision-making.

How AI is Revolutionizing Investment Strategies

Artificial intelligence has ushered in an era of data-driven decision-making that was previously unimaginable. Through sophisticated algorithms and advanced machine learning techniques, AI has the ability to analyze vast volumes of data at incredible speeds, extracting insights and patterns that human investors might overlook. This seismic shift allows investment professionals to make more informed decisions, leveraging data-driven predictions to maximize returns and minimize risks.

AI is also a masterful tool for spotting trends and anomalies within financial markets. It can detect subtle correlations and uncover hidden patterns that can guide investment strategies with a level of precision that was once considered unattainable. Additionally, AI can swiftly process news and global events, immediately assessing their potential impact on markets and making real-time adjustments accordingly.

Utilizing Robo-Advisors and Algorithmic Trading
The advent of robo-advisors has been a game-changer for investors seeking a streamlined, cost-effective approach to portfolio management. These AI-powered platforms assess an investor's risk tolerance, financial goals, and other parameters to generate personalized investment strategies. Robo-advisors construct and manage portfolios with minimal human intervention, leveraging algorithms to rebalance and optimize holdings as market conditions evolve.

Algorithmic trading, often referred to as algo-trading, takes automation a step further. This involves the execution of trades based on pre-defined criteria and rules. Algorithms can swiftly execute large volumes of trades across multiple markets, capitalizing on market inefficiencies and fleeting opportunities. This lightning-fast execution can also reduce the impact of emotional biases, a common pitfall for human traders.

Balancing Automation with Human Decision-Making
While the promise of AI and automation is undeniable, it's important to remember that these tools are not infallible. They lack the nuance of human judgment, and certain market conditions or unforeseen events can challenge their predictive capabilities. Therefore, a key challenge lies in

striking the right balance between automation and human oversight.

Human decision-making brings to the table a level of intuition, creativity, and contextual understanding that AI cannot replicate. Investors possess the ability to consider broader economic and geopolitical factors, which can significantly influence market dynamics. Moreover, the emotional intelligence humans bring—such as the capacity to factor in sentiment and respond to unexpected events— remains an invaluable asset.

To successfully integrate AI and automation into investment strategies, a hybrid approach is often recommended. This entails using AI to analyze data, generate insights, and propose strategies, while human experts provide oversight and adapt strategies based on their deep understanding of market nuances. It's a harmonious partnership—one that leverages the strengths of both human and machine intelligence.

The future of investing is undeniably intertwined with the evolution of AI and automation. These technologies are reshaping the landscape, offering investors unprecedented access to data-driven insights and efficient portfolio management. Robo-advisors and algorithmic trading are transforming how we approach investments, providing cost-effective and streamlined solutions. However, the delicate equilibrium between automation and human decision-making remains pivotal. By embracing a hybrid approach, investors can harness the power of AI while benefiting from the wisdom and intuition that humans uniquely offer. As we stand on the cusp of this exciting era, navigating the intersection of AI and investing will undoubtedly define the success of many in the financial world.

Chapter 6: Scaling Up Your Business Efforts

From Solopreneur to Business Owner

In the journey of entrepreneurship, there comes a point when the demands of your growing business surpass your individual capacity. The transition from a solopreneur, where you handle all aspects of your business single-handedly, to a business owner who orchestrates a team, marks a pivotal moment of growth. This phase not only tests your ability to relinquish control but also presents an opportunity to scale your enterprise to new heights. In this sub-chapter, we delve into the nuances of this transformation, exploring the art of delegating, establishing efficient systems, and maintaining quality while expanding your venture.

Delegating Tasks and Building a Team

The most profound leap from solopreneurship to business ownership involves assembling a team. Your first foray into delegation might be met with apprehension, as entrusting tasks to others can feel like a relinquishment of control. However, it's crucial to recognize that delegation is a strategic step towards achieving more substantial objectives.

Begin by identifying tasks that require your core expertise and direct involvement. These are the areas where your unique insights and skills have the most impact. Delegate operational and administrative tasks that can be executed effectively by others, allowing you to channel your energy into strategic decision-making.

Hiring the right individuals for your team is an art that requires alignment with your business's vision and culture. Seek candidates who possess skills that complement your strengths. Be transparent about your expectations and provide a clear outline of responsibilities. Regular communication and fostering an environment of collaboration will not only enhance productivity but also cultivate a sense of ownership among your team members.

Creating Systems and Processes for Efficiency
As your business expands, maintaining consistent quality becomes paramount. This is where systems and processes enter the equation. These frameworks serve as the backbone of your operations, ensuring that tasks are executed consistently, regardless of who is handling them.

Start by documenting every aspect of your business's workflow – from customer interactions to product development. This documentation lays the foundation for creating standardized processes. Establish clear guidelines, benchmarks, and performance metrics. This not only enhances efficiency but also facilitates smooth onboarding for new team members.

Automation tools and software can play a significant role in streamlining processes. Embrace technology to handle routine tasks, allowing your team to focus on more strategic activities. Regularly assess the effectiveness of your systems and remain open to refinements as your business evolves.

Balancing Growth While Maintaining Quality

Rapid expansion can sometimes lead to a trade-off between growth and quality. Ensuring that your business maintains the same level of excellence, or even improves it, during this phase requires strategic planning and a commitment to your core values.

First and foremost, communicate your vision and quality standards clearly to your team. Everyone should be aligned with the values that define your brand. Monitor the impact of growth on your customer experience – solicit feedback and be agile in making improvements.

Balancing growth also involves pacing your expansion efforts. Rapid hiring and aggressive scaling can strain your resources and dilute your focus. Consider your market's demand, the scalability of your operations, and the availability of capital before making expansion decisions.

The transition from solopreneur to business owner is a transformational journey that demands adaptability, strategic thinking, and a willingness to let go of micromanagement. Delegating tasks, building an efficient framework, and maintaining quality while growing are the key tenets of this transition. Remember, your role evolves from being the sole engine of your business to orchestrating a symphony of talented individuals working towards a common goal. As you embrace this evolution, you not only scale your business but also empower it to thrive in a dynamic marketplace.

International Expansion and Global Markets

In the dynamic landscape of modern business, growth and expansion often demand reaching beyond familiar horizons. The quest for global market presence has become a strategic imperative for businesses of all sizes. The process of international expansion, however, is rife with intricacies that require careful consideration and meticulous planning. In this sub chapter, we delve into the crucial steps and strategies necessary for successful global expansion.

Assessing the Potential of International Markets

Venturing into international markets begins with a comprehensive assessment of the potential they offer. A thorough market analysis involves evaluating factors such as the demand for your product or service, the competitive landscape, and the economic and regulatory environment of the target countries. One must also consider demographic and cultural aspects that may influence consumer behavior and preferences.

In this digital age, technological advancements have made market research more accessible. Companies can gather valuable data from online sources, social media, and market research firms to gain insights into consumer preferences, market trends, and emerging opportunities. It is essential to identify the markets that align with your business's strengths and values, ensuring that your expansion efforts are not only profitable but sustainable in the long run.

Adapting to Cultural and Regulatory Differences
Cultural nuances and regulatory variations can significantly
impact the success of your global expansion strategy.
Adapting to the cultural preferences and norms of the target
market is imperative to building strong relationships with
local consumers. This often involves tailoring your
marketing messages, product offerings, and even business
practices to align with the cultural sensibilities of the
region.

Additionally, navigating regulatory differences requires a
meticulous approach. International markets may have
distinct legal and regulatory frameworks that impact
aspects such as product certifications, intellectual property
rights, and business operations. Engaging local legal
experts and consultants can provide invaluable guidance to
ensure compliance with local laws and regulations.

Strategies for Successful Global Expansion
Successful global expansion hinges on a well-defined
strategy that encompasses both short-term goals and long-
term vision. Here are key strategies to consider:

1. Market Entry Method: Choose the most suitable
market entry method based on the nature of your business
and the target market. Options range from direct exports
and joint ventures to franchising and establishing wholly-
owned subsidiaries.

2. Localization: Customize your products, services, and
marketing strategies to resonate with the local culture. This

involves more than just translating content; it requires a deep understanding of cultural norms and preferences.

3. Distribution Networks: Establish efficient distribution networks that cater to the unique logistical challenges of the target market. An effective supply chain ensures timely delivery and customer satisfaction.

4. Talent Acquisition: Build a diverse and skilled workforce that understands the local market intricacies. Hiring local talent can provide insights and connections crucial for success.

5. Adaptive Marketing: Craft marketing campaigns that resonate with the local audience while maintaining your brand's core identity. Cultural sensitivity and local relevance are key.

6. Risk Mitigation: Diversify your risks by entering multiple markets rather than relying solely on one. This strategy can provide a buffer against economic fluctuations or political uncertainties in specific regions.

7. Continuous Learning: Stay attuned to the evolving market dynamics and consumer behaviors in each market you enter. Flexibility and adaptability are crucial in an ever-changing global landscape.

In essence, global expansion demands a well-informed, agile, and culturally sensitive approach. Success in international markets is not solely determined by the size of the business but by the depth of understanding and preparedness to navigate the complexities of diverse markets.

Expanding into global markets is a transformative journey that requires a blend of strategic thinking, cultural awareness, and adaptability. As your business steps onto the international stage, remember that each market presents its unique opportunities and challenges. With meticulous planning and a commitment to understanding and respecting the cultures you engage with, your business can truly thrive in the global arena.

Building a Legacy: Succession Planning

In the realm of business, the true mark of a visionary entrepreneur lies not only in their ability to scale their company during their tenure but also in their foresight to ensure its sustained success long after their departure. This pivotal process is known as succession planning – a meticulous strategy that secures the continuity of a business, preserves its values, and empowers future leaders to carry forward the mission.

Ensuring Business Continuity Beyond Your Involvement

One of the most significant challenges that growing businesses face is the prospect of leadership transition. A successful entrepreneur recognizes that their legacy extends far beyond their personal contributions. As a result, succession planning becomes a paramount consideration. It involves the strategic transfer of leadership and decision-making responsibilities to qualified individuals who possess the acumen to navigate challenges and seize opportunities.

The first step in this process is identifying the most suitable successors. This selection is not merely about finding skilled professionals but also aligning them with the company's culture and values. The potential successors should be individuals who share the original founder's vision and are dedicated to upholding the organization's mission.

Once identified, a comprehensive plan is developed to ensure a seamless transition. This plan encompasses the transfer of knowledge, relationships, and responsibilities. It involves grooming the successors through mentorship, strategic exposure, and hands-on experience. By imparting insights garnered over years of experience, the departing leader equips their successors with the wisdom required to make informed decisions.

Identifying and Grooming Future Leaders
The core of effective succession planning lies in the meticulous grooming of potential leaders. This extends beyond the development of technical skills. It entails honing qualities such as emotional intelligence, strategic thinking, and the ability to manage complex situations. The successors must be capable not only of managing day-to-day operations but also of guiding the company toward new horizons.

In many cases, an experienced entrepreneur will take an active role in mentoring their successors. This mentorship provides invaluable insights into navigating challenges, building relationships, and maintaining the organization's reputation. As a mentor, the founder transfers not only knowledge but also their passion and commitment to the business's success.

Furthermore, this grooming process often involves exposing successors to various aspects of the business. This holistic approach ensures that they understand the intricate dynamics, from customer interactions to supply chain management. By familiarizing themselves with every facet, future leaders gain a comprehensive perspective that aids in well-informed decision-making.

Preserving Your Business's Values and Mission
The most enduring companies are those that remain true to their founding principles. When transitioning leadership, preserving the company's values and mission becomes a non-negotiable priority. The vision that inspired the organization's inception should continue to be the driving force guiding its evolution.

This continuity is achieved through a blend of deliberate efforts. Documenting the company's core values, principles, and long-term goals creates a blueprint for future leaders to follow. In addition, fostering a culture that embraces these values and aligns with the business's mission serves as a beacon for everyone within the organization.

As the torch passes to the next generation of leaders, it is essential that they understand and embrace the legacy they are entrusted with. Encouraging open communication between departing and incoming leaders helps facilitate a smooth transition. This dialogue allows for the transfer of insights, concerns, and aspirations, fostering mutual respect and trust.

Succession planning is a testament to an entrepreneur's dedication to their business's longevity. It is an investment in the future – a commitment to ensuring that the enterprise thrives under new leadership. By identifying and nurturing future leaders, and by ingraining the company's values and mission into its DNA, a business can transcend the boundaries of time, leaving an indelible mark on industries, communities, and generations to come.

Chapter 7: The Power of Intellectual Property

Monetizing Your Knowledge through Information Products

In today's digitally-driven era, the art of monetizing your expertise through information products has emerged as a pivotal avenue for generating substantial passive income streams. This subchapter delves deeper into the intricacies of transforming your knowledge into valuable courses and workshops that cater to a hungry audience, while simultaneously safeguarding your intellectual property rights and employing effective marketing strategies to amplify the reach of your offerings.

Creating Valuable Courses and Workshops

The process of crafting a compelling information product begins with pinpointing a subject that not only aligns with your expertise but also fulfills a genuine need within your niche. This entails thorough research to gain a profound understanding of the pain points and challenges that your potential customers grapple with. Armed with this insight, you can artfully structure your content to provide actionable insights, step-by-step guidance, and real-world examples that empower your learners to tangibly progress in their journeys.

As you embark on the journey of content creation, consider the diverse learning preferences of your audience. To effectively cater to different learning styles, integrate a range of resources. This might encompass dynamic video lectures, interactive quizzes that reinforce learning, downloadable resources like cheat sheets and templates, and practical exercises that bridge the gap between theory and application. This multifaceted approach enhances comprehension, engagement, and retention, ensuring that your learners derive genuine value from your offerings.

Protecting Your Intellectual Property Rights
As you invest substantial effort and creativity into crafting your information products, it becomes imperative to safeguard your intellectual property rights. This measure ensures that the value you've painstakingly built isn't diluted or exploited by unauthorized parties. Depending on the nature of your content, consider exploring legal protections such as trademarking your brand name, copyrighting written materials, and potentially seeking patents if your offerings involve unique methodologies, proprietary tools, or innovative technology.

In conjunction with legal safeguards, the strategic licensing of your content reinforces your control over its utilization. Employ mechanisms that allow access only to individuals who have legitimately purchased or gained access to your products. This not only preserves your content's value but also fosters a sense of exclusivity that can heighten its appeal.

Marketing and Selling Your Information Products Effectively

Creating top-notch content is merely the starting point; effective marketing and sales strategies are the conduits through which your products reach their intended audience. Start by cultivating a robust online presence, which includes a professional website, active engagement on social media platforms, and a well-organized email marketing strategy. The goal is to ensure that potential customers encounter your offerings seamlessly across multiple touch points.

Crafting persuasive sales pages is an art in itself. These pages should articulate the unique value your information products offer, outlining the benefits that learners can expect and offering glimpses into the transformational journey they are embarking upon. Accompanying visual elements and compelling copy can paint a vivid picture of the value your products bring to the table.

Testimonials and case studies serve as powerful tools for substantiating the effectiveness of your offerings. By showcasing real-world success stories and the positive impact your products have had on previous customers, you instill trust and credibility within your prospective audience.

Diversifying your pricing options caters to a broader range of budgets. Consider tiered pricing structures that grant different levels of access and benefits, allowing customers to choose the option that best suits their needs and financial capacity.

Furthermore, forming strategic alliances with influencers or affiliates in your industry can amplify your reach significantly. By leveraging the existing audiences of these trusted figures, you gain access to a wider demographic that's predisposed to trust recommendations from figures they admire.

Consistent evaluation and optimization of your marketing strategies are pivotal. Leverage data analytics to track sales metrics, monitor customer engagement, and discern patterns in user behavior. This empirical insight facilitates data-driven decision-making, enabling you to refine your approach for maximum impact.

The journey from intellectual capital to profitable information products is multifaceted and demanding. By meticulously crafting valuable content, securing your intellectual property, and executing potent marketing strategies, you set the stage for the successful monetization of your expertise. Always bear in mind that the bridge between idea and income requires unwavering dedication, strategic planning, and an unceasing commitment to delivering value to your audience.

Licensing and Syndication for Content Creators
In today's rapidly evolving digital landscape, content creation has emerged as a potent tool for generating income and establishing a brand. As a content creator, your work

possesses inherent value that extends beyond its immediate reach. The strategic exploration of licensing and syndication opportunities enables you to harness the full potential of your creations, optimizing revenue streams and expanding your audience outreach.

Exploring Licensing Opportunities for Your Content
Licensing your content involves granting permission to others to use your intellectual property under specified terms and conditions. This can encompass a wide range of materials, including written works, images, videos, software, and more. Licensing offers a remarkable avenue for monetization, as you maintain ownership of your content while permitting others to use it for various purposes.

When considering licensing opportunities, it's essential to identify the scope and nature of usage that aligns with your content's purpose and your brand's values. This could encompass limited rights for specific uses, such as educational materials, marketing campaigns, or merchandise. Careful selection of licensees and adherence to legal frameworks ensure that your content remains protected while contributing to your revenue generation strategy.

Syndicating Your Work Across Various Platforms
Syndication involves distributing your content across different platforms to maximize its reach and impact.

Syndication takes advantage of various media outlets, websites, and networks to amplify the exposure of your content to broader audiences. It's a powerful approach for boosting brand visibility and fostering engagement.

By syndicating your work, you tap into the audiences of established platforms, effectively capitalizing on their readership or viewership. Syndication often involves adapting your content to suit the style and tone of the platform while retaining the core message and value. This adaptive approach ensures that your content resonates with the new audience while maintaining its authenticity.

Negotiating Favorable Deals and Contracts
Navigating the world of licensing and syndication demands adept negotiation skills to secure favorable deals and contracts. These agreements outline the terms under which your content will be used and how compensation will be structured. Negotiations encompass a range of considerations, including usage rights, duration of usage, compensation models, and exclusivity clauses.

As a content creator, your goal should be to strike a balance between revenue generation and maintaining your content's integrity. Negotiating favorable terms involves meticulous attention to detail, understanding industry standards, and asserting your rights as the creator. Engaging with legal experts who specialize in intellectual property can greatly assist in ensuring that contracts are equitable and legally sound.

In the dynamic landscape of digital content, the potential for income generation through licensing and syndication is vast. Embracing these opportunities not only enhances your revenue streams but also enables your work to reach new corners of the digital world. However, as you venture into licensing and syndication, it's paramount to uphold the quality and consistency of your content, maintaining the essence that defines your brand.

Licensing and syndication are powerful tools that empower content creators to expand their horizons and tap into new avenues of revenue. By thoughtfully exploring licensing opportunities, skillfully syndicating across platforms, and adeptly negotiating contracts, content creators can unlock the full potential of their intellectual property. This strategic approach not only contributes to financial success but also solidifies your position in the digital realm as a distinguished creator with a lasting impact.

Writing and Publishing Books for Passive Income

In the modern world of entrepreneurship, where diversification and creativity reign supreme, one avenue that has proven to be a powerful source of both passive income and personal brand enhancement is writing and self-publishing books. The process of crafting a book, strategically marketing it, and converting it into a steady stream of income is a journey that requires careful planning, persistent effort, and a deep understanding of the evolving publishing landscape.

The Process of Writing and Self-Publishing Books
Creating a book that resonates with your target audience and establishes your expertise requires a blend of passion, discipline, and a structured approach. Before diving into the writing process, it's crucial to define your book's purpose, audience, and core message. This initial groundwork will serve as your compass throughout the writing journey.

1. Conceptualization and Planning: Begin by brainstorming ideas and identifying the unique value you can offer to readers. Craft a compelling book concept that addresses a specific problem or need in your target market. Outline your book's structure, chapters, and key points to maintain a clear direction during the writing process.

2. Writing Strategy: Establish a writing routine that suits your schedule and creative flow. Some authors prefer to set daily word count goals, while others allocate specific time slots for writing. Consistency is key – make progress each day to maintain momentum.

3. Crafting Engaging Content: Your writing should be informative, engaging, and well-researched. Support your insights with relevant data, anecdotes, and examples. Strive for a balance between depth and readability, catering to both beginners and those well-versed in the subject.

4. Editing and Refinement: After completing the initial draft, take a step back before diving into editing. Revise for clarity, coherence, and grammar. Consider seeking professional editing services to ensure your book meets high-quality standards.

5. Design and Formatting: A visually appealing book layout enhances the reading experience. If self-publishing digitally, invest in professional formatting that adapts well to various devices and screens.

Marketing Strategies to Reach a Wider Audience
Once your manuscript is polished and ready, the next step is to introduce it to the world. Effective marketing is vital for reaching a wider audience and generating sales. Leveraging various platforms and strategies can significantly boost your book's visibility:

1. Building Pre-Launch Buzz: Create anticipation before the official launch. Tease your audience with snippets, behind-the-scenes content, and even pre-order options.

2. Leveraging Social Media: Engage your existing followers and tap into relevant online communities. Share valuable insights related to your book's topic, gradually building a loyal audience.

3. Author Website and Blog: Establish a professional author website where readers can learn more about you and your book. Maintain a blog that offers value and showcases your expertise.

4. Email Marketing: Start building an email list early on. Send regular updates, exclusive content, and promotional offers to keep your audience engaged.

5. Collaborations and Influencers: Partner with influencers or experts in your field who can endorse your book to their audience. This can significantly expand your reach and credibility.

Turning Your Books into a Steady Income Source
Publishing a book isn't just about sharing knowledge; it's also an avenue for creating a sustainable income stream. Here are strategies to monetize your book effectively:

1. Choosing the Right Pricing Strategy: Pricing plays a crucial role in attracting readers while ensuring you earn a reasonable return. Consider factors such as production costs, perceived value, and market competition.

2. Digital and Print Distribution: Opt for both digital (e-book) and print formats to cater to different reader preferences. Utilize platforms like Google Play Book and IngramSpark for distribution.

3. Royalties and Revenue Streams: Understand the royalty structure of different publishing platforms. Explore options for exclusive and non-exclusive distribution to maximize earnings.

4. Upselling and Cross-Promotion: Include calls-to-action within your book that direct readers to your other products or services. This could be an online course, consulting services, or additional books.

5. Maintaining Consistency: Consider writing a series or follow-up books to keep readers engaged and coming back for more.

Writing and publishing books offers a multifaceted opportunity to showcase your expertise, provide value to readers, and generate passive income. By meticulously crafting your content, strategically marketing your work, and optimizing revenue streams, you can transform your book into a consistent source of income while making a lasting impact on your audience. Remember, the journey of a successful author requires continuous learning, adaptation, and an unwavering commitment to excellence.

Chapter 8: Mindful Wealth Management

Achieving Financial Independence and Early Retirement

In the ever-evolving landscape of personal finance, the concept of Financial Independence, Retire Early (FIRE) has emerged as a guiding philosophy for those seeking a new level of financial freedom and control over their lives. This subchapter delves into the depths of FIRE, exploring its core principles, the strategies to achieve it, and the intricate process of transitioning to an early retirement while ensuring lasting financial stability.

The Concept of FIRE (Financial Independence, Retire Early)

FIRE isn't merely an acronym; it embodies a profound shift in how individuals perceive their relationship with money and work. At its essence, FIRE represents a commitment to achieving financial independence, allowing individuals to break free from the traditional 9-to-5 grind and gain the flexibility to live life on their own terms. However, achieving FIRE isn't about quitting work altogether; it's about cultivating a life where work becomes optional, and financial worries are no longer a primary concern.

Strategies for Aggressive Saving and Investment

The foundation of the FIRE movement is built upon a disciplined approach to saving and investing. FIRE enthusiasts often embrace a minimalist lifestyle, focusing on needs rather than wants and channeling the savings into investments that have the potential to grow exponentially. Central to this strategy is the idea of "lean FIRE" and "fat FIRE." Lean FIRE aims for early retirement with a frugal lifestyle, while fat FIRE allows for a more comfortable lifestyle post-retirement.

Aggressive saving is the cornerstone of FIRE. It entails not only controlling spending habits but also consciously allocating a significant portion of one's income to investments. This may involve cutting unnecessary expenses, renegotiating recurring bills, and scrutinizing every financial decision for alignment with long-term goals.

Transitioning to Retirement While Maintaining Financial Stability

Transitioning to early retirement requires meticulous planning to ensure financial stability and longevity. As you bid farewell to the corporate world, it's imperative to have a clear blueprint that addresses various aspects, from healthcare and insurance coverage to sustainable income streams.

Healthcare is a critical consideration, especially in countries with complex healthcare systems. Many early retirees opt for Health Savings Accounts (HSAs) and bridge insurance options to safeguard against unexpected medical expenses.

Moreover, the transition phase involves a shift in investment strategy. As the reliance on earned income diminishes, the focus turns toward generating passive income. A well-diversified portfolio of stocks, bonds, real estate, and perhaps even side businesses can provide a consistent revenue stream without depleting the principal.

Emotional preparedness is equally important. Early retirees must navigate the psychological shift from being defined by their careers to embracing new identities. Many find purpose and engagement through volunteer work, pursuing hobbies, or even launching passion projects that align with their interests.

The FIRE movement is a testament to the evolving dynamics of personal finance. It challenges conventional notions of retirement, encouraging individuals to embark on a journey of financial independence, pursuing passions, and crafting lives of purpose. While achieving FIRE demands rigorous dedication, meticulous planning, and strategic investments, the reward is a life that revolves around meaningful experiences rather than the constraints of financial obligations. By embracing the principles of FIRE, individuals can pave their way toward early retirement without compromising their financial stability or sacrificing their aspirations.

Philanthropy and Giving Back

In the pursuit of wealth creation and financial success, one must not overlook the profound impact that philanthropy and giving back can have on both individual fulfillment and societal progress. While accumulating wealth is a significant goal, using that wealth to effect positive change is equally important. This subchapter delves into the world of philanthropy, exploring how incorporating charitable giving into your financial plan can create a lasting legacy and strike a balance between financial goals and social impact.

Incorporating Charitable Giving into Your Financial Plan

True mindful wealth management involves recognizing the responsibility that accompanies financial success. Incorporating charitable giving into your financial plan isn't just a matter of allocating funds; it's a conscious decision to contribute to causes that resonate with your values and passions. Charitable giving isn't solely about the monetary aspect; it's about aligning your resources with causes that matter to you.

Begin by identifying areas or issues that hold personal significance. Whether it's education, healthcare, poverty alleviation, environmental conservation, or any other cause, your giving should be a reflection of your core values. Research and engage with reputable nonprofit organizations that are actively making a difference in those areas. Consider setting aside a percentage of your income or investment returns specifically for charitable purposes.

This commitment creates a structured approach to giving, ensuring that it remains an integral part of your financial journey.

Creating a Legacy through Philanthropic Efforts
Philanthropy provides a remarkable opportunity to create a lasting legacy that extends beyond financial transactions. It's a chance to leave a positive mark on the world, influencing lives and inspiring future generations. By actively engaging in philanthropic efforts, you lay the foundation for a legacy rooted in compassion and positive change.

Consider establishing a family foundation or donor-advised fund to formalize your philanthropic endeavors. These structures provide a platform for involving your family and passing down the values of giving. Engage your loved ones in discussions about the causes you support, fostering a shared sense of purpose and responsibility.

Balancing Financial Goals with Social Impact
Philanthropy should be seen not as a trade-off against financial goals, but as a complementary component of a holistic wealth management strategy. The perception that giving back diminishes financial growth is a misconception; in fact, strategic philanthropy can enhance your reputation, network, and even business opportunities.

Balancing financial goals with social impact requires thoughtful planning. Integrate your giving strategy into your financial plan, allocating a portion of your resources to philanthropy while still pursuing your financial aspirations. This equilibrium fosters a sense of fulfillment, as the wealth you generate is put to meaningful use beyond personal gain.

As your wealth grows, consider expanding your philanthropic efforts. Collaborate with like-minded individuals, participate in community initiatives, and explore innovative solutions to societal challenges. Your philanthropic journey can evolve over time, adapting to changes in your financial situation and the evolving needs of society.

Incorporating charitable giving into your financial plan is a testament to your commitment to making a positive impact. It's an acknowledgement of the interconnectedness of wealth and social responsibility. By aligning your financial goals with meaningful philanthropic efforts, you create a legacy that transcends generations, leaving behind a world that's better for your contributions. Mindful wealth management is not solely about the accumulation of riches; it's about utilizing those riches to make a lasting difference in the lives of others and in the world as a whole.

Navigating Financial Windfalls and Windfalls

In the journey towards achieving financial success and security, one of the most exciting yet challenging scenarios that individuals may encounter is the sudden influx of wealth. These windfalls, whether through inheritance, unexpected business success, a significant investment payoff, or even a lottery win, can present a unique set of opportunities and complexities. Navigating such situations with prudence and wisdom is paramount to ensuring that newfound wealth becomes a lasting legacy rather than a fleeting experience.

Managing Sudden Wealth with Prudence

The allure of sudden wealth can often trigger impulsive decisions and unchecked spending. It's essential to approach this newfound prosperity with a sense of prudence and a clear understanding of your financial goals. While it might be tempting to indulge in extravagant purchases or investments, taking a step back and assessing the bigger picture is crucial.

First and foremost, establishing a comprehensive financial plan becomes paramount. This plan should encompass short-term needs, long-term goals, and a solid strategy for wealth preservation. Allocating a portion of the windfall towards clearing debts, creating an emergency fund, and investing in diverse assets can provide a solid foundation for ongoing financial security.

Furthermore, wise financial stewardship involves seeking a balance between enjoying the benefits of newfound wealth

and securing it for the future. Taking a measured approach
to spending ensures that immediate desires do not
compromise long-term stability.

Seeking Professional Advice and Guidance
Navigating the complexities of substantial wealth requires
expertise that extends beyond personal financial
knowledge. Consulting professionals, such as financial
advisors, tax specialists, and estate planners, can provide
invaluable guidance in making informed decisions.

A financial advisor can help develop a tailored investment
strategy that aligns with your risk tolerance and financial
objectives. They can also provide insights into tax-efficient
investment options, potentially reducing the tax burden on
your windfall.

In situations involving substantial wealth, estate planning
takes on added significance. Establishing or updating a
will, setting up trusts, and addressing potential estate tax
implications are crucial steps that professionals in this field
can assist with. Their expertise ensures that your wealth is
distributed in accordance with your wishes while
minimizing potential legal complications.

Preserving Wealth for the Long Term
Preserving newfound wealth for the long term requires a
disciplined and strategic approach. While immediate
opportunities may seem enticing, the real measure of

success lies in the ability to generate sustainable and lasting income.

Diversification remains a cornerstone principle of wealth preservation. Spreading investments across different asset classes, such as stocks, bonds, real estate, and alternative investments, mitigates risk and enhances the potential for consistent returns. A diversified portfolio also positions your wealth to weather market fluctuations.

Beyond investments, developing a culture of financial literacy within your family is essential. Educating your loved ones about prudent financial management ensures that the legacy you've built continues to thrive across generations. Open conversations about wealth, philanthropy, and responsible stewardship can foster a sense of responsibility and shared purpose.

The windfalls of wealth offer both unprecedented opportunities and challenges. Through a combination of prudent management, professional guidance, and a commitment to preserving wealth for the long term, individuals can transform sudden prosperity into a legacy that shapes their lives and the lives of future generations. Taking the time to understand the intricacies of financial windfalls and navigating them with wisdom is a testament to the power of mindful wealth management.

Chapter 9: Risk Management and Resilience

Insurance Strategies for Wealth Protection

In the intricate tapestry of financial success and wealth creation, there lies a critical thread that often remains overlooked until it's needed most – insurance. Just as a skilled sailor anticipates storms at sea, astute financial planners recognize the importance of insurance in safeguarding their hard-earned assets against unexpected challenges. In this sub-chapter, we delve into the realm of insurance strategies for wealth protection, exploring the nuances of different insurance types, the art of tailoring coverage, and the profound role insurance plays in mitigating financial risks.

Understanding Different Types of Insurance

Insurance, in its various forms, acts as a shield against the unpredictable, providing a safety net that cushions the impact of life's adversities. From health to property, life to liability, there exists an array of insurance categories, each designed to address specific risks.

Health Insurance: This cornerstone of insurance covers medical expenses, offering financial relief when health issues arise. It not only ensures access to quality healthcare but also shields individuals and families from the exorbitant costs associated with medical treatments, hospitalizations, and prescription medications.

Property Insurance: Unforeseen events such as natural disasters, accidents, or theft can wreak havoc on property owners. Property insurance safeguards against damage or loss of physical assets, such as homes or businesses. It provides financial support to rebuild and recover, allowing individuals and business owners to restore their lives and operations.

Life Insurance: Life insurance stands as a beacon of protection for loved ones in the event of a policyholder's passing. It ensures that financial obligations and aspirations endure even in absence. For families, life insurance guarantees continued financial stability, covering outstanding debts, mortgage payments, and funding future endeavors such as education or retirement.

Liability Insurance: Accidents and unforeseen events can lead to legal claims against individuals or businesses. Liability insurance shields policyholders from the financial fallout of such claims, covering legal expenses, settlements, and judgments. It is a vital component for individuals and businesses alike, offering a layer of protection against potential financial ruin.

Tailoring Insurance Coverage to Your Needs

The art of crafting a comprehensive insurance strategy lies in its customization to align with your specific needs and risk tolerance. While insurance offers a safety net, over-insuring can lead to unnecessary expenses, while under-insuring leaves you exposed to unforeseen liabilities.

When selecting health insurance, for instance, consider factors such as your medical history, family needs, and preferred healthcare providers. A family with young children might prioritize comprehensive coverage that includes pediatric care and preventive services. Conversely, a young and healthy individual might opt for a plan with a higher deductible to minimize premium costs.

When insuring property, factor in location-specific risks and potential damages that might not be covered by standard policies. For properties located in flood-prone areas, securing additional flood insurance can be essential, as standard property insurance typically does not cover flood-related damages.

When contemplating life insurance, gauge your dependents' financial requirements and long-term goals. If you have young children, consider a policy that can provide for their education and future needs. If you have dependents with special needs, a life insurance policy can ensure their ongoing care and financial security.

Mitigating Financial Risks through Insurance
Insurance is not merely a financial instrument; it is a tool of resilience, offering protection against the unexpected. Beyond safeguarding assets, insurance brings peace of mind, allowing you to focus on your wealth-building endeavors without the looming shadow of potential financial disasters.

In business ventures, insurance acts as a buffer against the uncertainties that come with entrepreneurship. Business insurance covers a range of risks, including property damage, liability, employee-related issues, and business interruption. By having the right insurance coverage in place, entrepreneurs can safeguard their investment and maintain business continuity, even in the face of unforeseen challenges.

Moreover, insurance is a mechanism that allows you to transfer the burden of risk to an entity equipped to handle it. When an unforeseen event strikes, insurance steps in to soften the blow, preventing a single setback from erasing years of diligent effort. This principle applies not only to individuals but also to businesses, providing stability and confidence in the face of uncertainties.

Insurance stands as an essential pillar of risk management and financial resilience. The intricate web of insurance categories offers tailored solutions to specific risks, protecting your health, assets, and financial aspirations. By customizing your insurance coverage to align with your needs and aspirations, you strike a balance between safeguarding against potential losses and ensuring financial prudence. In the vast landscape of wealth creation, insurance serves as a reliable companion, navigating the storms and uncertainties that life can bring. As you journey toward financial success, let insurance be your steadfast ally, fortifying your path to prosperity. By embracing insurance strategies for wealth protection, you secure not only your assets but also your peace of mind, empowering yourself to face the future with confidence and resilience.

Crisis Management and Business Continuity

In the ever-evolving landscape of business, one immutable truth remains: challenges and disruptions are inevitable. The mark of a truly successful enterprise lies not only in its ability to thrive during favorable times but also in its capacity to weather storms and emerge stronger on the other side. This is where crisis management and business continuity strategies come into play. In this subchapter, we delve into the meticulous process of developing a crisis response plan, ensuring seamless business continuity in times of upheaval, and the invaluable lessons that arise from setbacks.

Developing a Crisis Response Plan

A crisis response plan is the bedrock of a resilient organization. It's a blueprint that guides decision-making and actions when the unexpected strikes. An effective plan involves:

1. Risk Assessment and Scenario Planning: Begin by identifying potential risks that your business may face. These could range from natural disasters and cyberattacks to supply chain disruptions. Once you've identified these risks, craft scenarios that simulate how these events might unfold. This process enables you to proactively anticipate challenges.

2. Clear Roles and Responsibilities: Define who does what in a crisis. Establish a crisis management team with representatives from various departments, each responsible for specific tasks. Clarity of roles ensures swift and coordinated actions when crisis strikes.

3. Communication Protocols: Communication is paramount during a crisis. Outline how you'll disseminate information internally and externally. Provide guidelines for communicating with employees, customers, partners, and the media. Honesty, transparency, and consistency should underpin all communications.

4. Resource Allocation: Anticipate the resources—financial, human, and technical—that you might need during a crisis. Having a reserve fund and contingency contracts can make a significant difference in navigating turbulent times.

Ensuring Business Continuity During Disruptions
Business continuity is the lifeline that ensures an organization can continue its core functions and services even in the face of disruptions. Key elements include:

1. Backup Systems and Redundancy: Invest in robust IT infrastructure, redundant systems, and data backup solutions. These measures ensure that if one system fails, there's a backup to keep operations running smoothly.

2. Remote Work Readiness: The COVID-19 pandemic highlighted the importance of having the capability for remote work. Develop a comprehensive remote work policy that includes secure access to systems, communication tools, and clear expectations for remote employees.

3. Supplier and Partner Relationships: Foster strong relationships with suppliers and partners. Diversify your supplier base to mitigate risks associated with supply chain disruptions. Regular communication helps keep everyone aligned and prepared.

4. Test and Refine Plans: Conduct regular drills and simulations to test the effectiveness of your crisis response and business continuity plans. This not only identifies gaps but also ensures that your team is well-versed in executing the plans when needed.

Learning from Setbacks and Adapting to Change
Setbacks, though unwelcome, offer profound learning opportunities. Every crisis holds within it the seeds of growth and transformation. Here's how to capitalize on setbacks:

1. Post-Crisis Evaluation: After the dust settles, conduct a thorough evaluation of your crisis response. What worked? What could be improved? Use these insights to refine your crisis management plan.

2. Flexibility and Adaptability: A crisis underscores the importance of adaptability. Cultivate a culture that embraces change and innovation. Those who can pivot swiftly and creatively in response to challenges are better poised for long-term success.

3. Resilience as a Leadership Trait: Leaders who demonstrate resilience and grace under pressure inspire their teams. Foster a leadership style that encourages collaboration, empathy, and clear-headed decision-making during turbulent times.

4. Building Back Stronger: As you rebuild after a crisis, seize the opportunity to enhance your organization's strengths. Innovate, explore new avenues, and emerge as a stronger, more agile entity.

In the realm of business, turbulence is a certainty. But with a well-crafted crisis response plan, a commitment to business continuity, and the ability to learn from setbacks, your organization can not only navigate challenges but also thrive in their wake. Through crisis management and resilience, businesses evolve into more robust, adaptable, and successful entities, prepared to navigate the unpredictable currents of the business world.

Emotional Intelligence in Financial Decision-Making

In the intricate web of financial decisions, rationality often clashes with emotions. The realm of money management is not merely a numbers game; it's profoundly influenced by the emotional currents that underlie our choices. This subchapter delves into the critical concept of emotional intelligence in financial decision-making, exploring how recognizing and managing emotions can shape a healthier relationship with money and contribute to long-term success.

Recognizing Emotions' Role in Financial Choices
The process of making financial decisions, whether investing, spending, or saving, is rarely devoid of emotional influences. Emotions such as fear, greed, and excitement can sway judgments, leading to impulsive actions that might not align with long-term goals. Recognizing the emotional triggers behind financial decisions is the first step towards mastering emotional intelligence.

Understanding the source of emotions is vital. For instance, fear of missing out (FOMO) can drive hasty investment choices, while the fear of loss might cause an individual to avoid investing altogether. Recognizing these emotional drivers allows us to step back, assess our motivations, and make more informed decisions.

Developing Emotional Resilience and Discipline
Emotional resilience is the ability to withstand and adapt to emotional challenges, a quality particularly relevant in financial matters. Market volatility, economic downturns, and unexpected expenses can all trigger emotional turmoil. Developing emotional resilience involves building a mindset that is prepared for uncertainties and equipped to rebound from setbacks.

Discipline plays a pivotal role in emotional resilience. Creating a structured financial plan and adhering to it, even in the face of emotional impulses, can act as a buffer against impulsive decisions. This discipline can prevent emotional extremes from derailing long-term strategies. By recognizing that emotions are transient and that market fluctuations are natural, individuals can build the mental fortitude needed to weather financial storms.

Cultivating a Healthy Relationship with Money
The relationship one holds with money often mirrors broader emotional patterns. For some, money may be associated with security, while for others, it symbolizes freedom or even self-worth. Developing emotional intelligence involves detangling these associations to foster a healthier relationship with money.

To cultivate a healthy relationship with money, it's crucial to separate self-worth from net worth. Placing one's value solely on financial success can lead to emotional distress in times of loss. Instead, understanding that money is a tool to achieve goals and live a fulfilling life allows for a more balanced perspective.

Moreover, practicing gratitude for the financial resources available, regardless of their scale, can shift the focus from what's lacking to what's abundant. This shift in perspective contributes to emotional well-being and reduces the anxiety often tied to financial matters.

Emotional intelligence is an indispensable skill in financial decision-making. It requires introspection, self-awareness, and discipline to navigate the emotional landscape that accompanies financial choices. By recognizing emotions' role, cultivating emotional resilience, and nurturing a healthy relationship with money, individuals can make decisions that align with their long-term objectives, thereby fostering financial success and peace of mind.

Chapter 10: Tax Strategies and Wealth Preservation

Tax-Efficient Investing and Asset Protection

Taxation and wealth preservation are integral aspects of any successful financial plan. As we navigate the complex world of finance, understanding how to minimize investment-related taxes and shield assets from risks and liabilities becomes paramount. In this sub chapter, we delve into the realm of tax-efficient investing and asset protection, unveiling strategies that not only optimize your financial outcomes but also safeguard your hard-earned wealth.

Strategies to Minimize Investment-Related Taxes

Tax efficiency is more than just a buzzword; it's a critical component of maximizing your investment returns. By strategically structuring your investments, you can reduce the impact of taxes on your portfolio. One such approach is asset location – allocating investments based on their tax treatment. This means placing tax-inefficient assets, like bonds generating regular interest, in tax-advantaged accounts, and tax-efficient assets, such as stocks, in taxable accounts. This simple yet powerful technique can lead to substantial tax savings over time.

Additionally, tax-loss harvesting is a proactive strategy that involves selling underperforming investments to offset capital gains and reduce your tax liability. This maneuver not only helps you mitigate taxes but also allows you to reposition your portfolio for potential future gains.

Shielding Assets from Potential Risks and Liabilities
Preserving wealth isn't just about growing your investments; it's also about safeguarding them from unforeseen risks and liabilities. Establishing legal structures, such as trusts and limited liability companies (LLCs), can provide a protective barrier around your assets. Trusts offer benefits like controlling the distribution of assets, minimizing estate taxes, and shielding assets from creditors. Similarly, forming an LLC for your real estate or business holdings can isolate those assets from your personal liabilities, reducing the potential impact of legal disputes or financial setbacks.

Another effective strategy is utilizing insurance products. Umbrella insurance, for instance, provides an extra layer of liability coverage beyond what your primary policies offer. This can safeguard your assets in case of lawsuits or liability claims that exceed your other insurance limits.

Seeking Professional Tax Advice for Optimal Results
While the world of tax-efficient investing and asset protection offers numerous strategies, the complexity of tax codes and legal nuances requires expert guidance. Seeking professional tax advice is an investment in itself, as qualified tax advisors can tailor strategies to your unique financial situation.

A certified tax professional can help you optimize your tax planning by identifying deductions, credits, and opportunities that might otherwise go unnoticed. Moreover, they can guide you through intricate legal procedures, ensuring that you navigate tax regulations and asset protection laws compliantly.

In the pursuit of building and preserving wealth, understanding the intricate interplay between taxation and asset protection is crucial. Tax-efficient investing strategies not only enhance your returns but also position you to weather market volatility with resilience. Shielding your assets from potential risks and liabilities safeguards your financial well-being for generations to come. And by seeking the counsel of experienced tax advisors, you can craft a comprehensive financial plan that reflects your aspirations and secures your financial future.

Estate Planning for Generational Wealth

Estate planning stands as a beacon at the intersection of financial strategy and emotional foresight. It is a deliberate and thoughtful endeavor that transcends generations, fostering the seamless transition of wealth, values, and legacy from one era to the next. In this subchapter, we delve into the intricacies of estate planning, unpacking its significance, and offering guidance on crafting a comprehensive plan that ensures the preservation of generational wealth.

Understanding the Importance of Estate Planning

Estate planning is not merely the arrangement of assets; it is the orchestration of a symphony that harmonizes one's financial aspirations with their familial aspirations. A well-crafted estate plan encompasses not only tangible assets but also intangible wealth such as values, traditions, and knowledge.

At its core, estate planning is an exercise in control and intentionality. By outlining your wishes regarding the distribution of assets, healthcare decisions, and even the guardianship of dependents, you ensure that your desires are respected even when you're no longer present to voice them.

However, estate planning transcends the personal realm. It's a mechanism to mitigate potential conflicts and tensions among heirs, thereby preserving family unity. It's a blueprint for securing the financial well-being of your loved ones while minimizing the financial burdens that may arise upon your passing.

Crafting a Comprehensive Estate Plan

Creating an effective estate plan requires a meticulous approach, often involving legal professionals and financial advisors who specialize in this field. It begins with a clear inventory of your assets – financial accounts, real estate, investments, and even digital assets – alongside liabilities and debts. This comprehensive overview lays the foundation for prudent decision-making.

One of the key aspects of estate planning is the creation of a will. A will is a legal document that outlines how your assets will be distributed upon your death. It's also a platform to designate guardians for minor children, ensuring their well-being if the unexpected occurs.

Trusts, another essential element, offer more complex and flexible options. Revocable living trusts, for instance, allow assets to bypass probate, thus expediting the transfer process and maintaining privacy. Irrevocable trusts can be used for gifting assets to beneficiaries while potentially minimizing estate taxes.

Designating beneficiaries on accounts such as retirement plans, life insurance policies, and investment accounts is a straightforward yet critical step. These designations often supersede the instructions in a will, making them a potent tool for ensuring your assets flow smoothly to intended recipients.

Transferring Wealth While Minimizing Taxes and Conflicts

Estate taxes, often referred to as the "death tax," can erode a significant portion of your estate if not properly managed. Engaging in strategic tax planning can substantially mitigate this burden. For instance, gifting assets during your lifetime can help reduce the taxable value of your estate. An experienced advisor can guide you through the intricacies of tax laws, ensuring you make informed decisions.

Navigating the complexities of generational wealth transfer requires thoughtful consideration of potential conflicts. In many cases, disputes arise due to vague or disputed terms within a will or trust. Open and transparent communication with heirs can mitigate such issues. Moreover, involving your family in the estate planning process can ensure their understanding of your decisions, fostering unity and alignment with your intentions.

Estate planning is an embodiment of your values, a strategic financial tool, and a legacy that transcends your mortal presence. A comprehensive plan crafted with diligence and guided by experienced professionals can ensure the seamless transfer of wealth, the preservation of harmony among heirs, and the enduring realization of your aspirations. It is a gift to your loved ones, offering them not only financial security but also the priceless assurance that your legacy will persist for generations to come.

International Taxation and Offshore Strategies

In our increasingly interconnected world, where borders blur and markets transcend national boundaries, understanding the intricacies of international taxation and offshore financial strategies has become a paramount consideration for individuals and businesses alike. The convergence of globalization and technology has presented both opportunities and challenges, transforming the way wealth is managed and preserved. In this sub chapter, we delve into the nuances of international taxation and legitimate offshore financial strategies, shedding light on the complex realm of cross-border wealth management.

Navigating Tax Considerations in a Global Economy
The digital age has paved the way for a borderless economy, offering new avenues for investment, trade, and financial growth. However, this global landscape introduces a maze of tax regulations, treaties, and compliance obligations. As individuals and businesses venture beyond their home territories, they encounter varying tax jurisdictions and reporting requirements. Navigating this intricate web demands a deep understanding of international tax laws and regulations.

One fundamental principle of international taxation is the determination of tax residency. Depending on a country's rules, individuals may be considered tax residents based on factors such as the duration of stay, source of income, or citizenship. Corporations, too, must grapple with the concept of permanent establishment—a notion that defines when a business's activities within a foreign jurisdiction trigger tax liabilities.

Exploring Legitimate Offshore Financial Options
Legitimate offshore financial strategies can offer a toolkit of advantages that go beyond mere tax optimization. Offshore jurisdictions often boast robust financial infrastructures, confidentiality provisions, and a conducive environment for global trade. One notable attraction is the potential for asset protection, as offshore structures can shield assets from legal disputes and creditors in one's home country.

Offshore financial centers also provide flexibility in estate planning, allowing individuals to tailor their inheritance arrangements in accordance with their wishes. Trusts and foundations, common offshore vehicles, can ensure seamless wealth transfer while offering potential tax benefits.

Compliance and Legal Aspects of International Taxation
Amid the allure of offshore strategies, it is critical to emphasize that adhering to compliance and legal requirements is non-negotiable. Authorities across the globe are intensifying their efforts to combat tax evasion, money laundering, and other financial crimes. Therefore, transparency and adherence to international regulations are paramount.

Compliance encompasses a range of factors, including the proper disclosure of offshore accounts, assets, and income. Organizations and individuals must stay well-informed about the reporting obligations set forth by their home jurisdictions and the countries in which they operate. The exchange of financial information among governments, facilitated by initiatives like the Common Reporting Standard (CRS), ensures that tax authorities have access to comprehensive data, minimizing opportunities for evasion.

Moreover, engaging with qualified professionals—tax consultants, legal advisors, and financial planners—with expertise in international taxation can safeguard against unintentional breaches of the law.

The landscape of international taxation and offshore financial strategies is both complex and dynamic. As we navigate this terrain, it's imperative to recognize that legitimate offshore approaches can provide substantial benefits, from asset protection to enhanced estate planning. However, compliance and adherence to legal requirements are integral to preserving the integrity of one's financial endeavors. The intricacies of international taxation demand a multifaceted approach—one that combines a solid understanding of tax laws, meticulous compliance, and the guidance of experts well-versed in this intricate domain. In embracing these principles, individuals and businesses can strategically manage their wealth in the global arena while staying firmly within the bounds of legality and ethical conduct.

Chapter 11: Embracing Technological Advancements

Fintech and Digital Payment Solutions

The digital revolution has ushered in a new era of convenience and efficiency in financial transactions. Fintech, short for financial technology, has rapidly transformed the landscape of how we manage, spend, and invest our money. From digital wallets to payment platforms, the realm of fintech has woven a tapestry of innovation that has redefined the way we interact with our finances. In this subchapter, we'll delve into the intricacies of fintech and explore the ways it has revolutionized the financial world.

Utilizing Digital Wallets and Payment Platforms

Digital wallets, once a futuristic concept, have become an integral part of our financial routines. A digital wallet, often referred to as an e-wallet, is a secure virtual container that holds various forms of digital assets, such as credit and debit card information, cryptocurrencies, and loyalty program points. These wallets streamline the payment process by allowing users to make transactions with a simple tap or click, eliminating the need to carry physical cards or cash.

Digital wallets offer a myriad of benefits. They provide unparalleled convenience, allowing users to make quick payments on e-commerce websites, in physical stores, or even between individuals. Moreover, they can store multiple payment methods, making it easy to switch between cards or funding sources. This simplicity is especially valuable for those who travel frequently or need to manage various financial accounts.

Enhancing Financial Transactions through Fintech
Fintech innovations go beyond just facilitating payments; they encompass a range of technologies that enhance the overall financial experience. One remarkable example is the integration of artificial intelligence (AI) and machine learning (ML) in fraud detection. These technologies analyze patterns of transactions and behaviors to identify unusual activities, providing an additional layer of security for digital transactions.

Moreover, fintech has democratized access to financial services. Many individuals who were previously excluded from traditional banking systems now have the opportunity to participate in the economy through mobile banking apps and digital lending platforms. This has been especially impactful in developing countries, where access to physical bank branches is limited.

Balancing Convenience and Security in Digital Finance
While the convenience of fintech is undeniable, the question of security often looms in the minds of users. It's essential to strike a balance between seamless transactions and safeguarding sensitive financial information. To address this, fintech companies have implemented robust

encryption techniques and multi-factor authentication processes.

One notable breakthrough in securing digital transactions is blockchain technology. Originally developed to underpin cryptocurrencies like Bitcoin, blockchain has transcended its origins to revolutionize various industries. Its decentralized and immutable nature has made it a formidable tool in ensuring the integrity and security of financial data. Blockchain's potential in transforming payment systems and record-keeping processes is immense, promising enhanced transparency and reduced fraud risks.

Fintech and digital payment solutions have not only streamlined financial transactions but have also paved the way for a more inclusive and secure financial ecosystem. As we embrace these technological advancements, it's crucial to remain vigilant about security practices while enjoying the benefits of convenience. The ever-evolving landscape of fintech continues to shape the way we manage our finances, providing a glimpse into a future where financial interactions are seamless, efficient, and accessible to all.

Automation and AI in Business Operations

Automation and artificial intelligence (AI) are reshaping the landscape of modern business operations. As we navigate the complexities of the digital age, embracing these technological advancements has become less of an option and more of a necessity. In this sub chapter, we delve into the transformative power of automation and AI, exploring how they streamline processes, drive data-driven decision-making, and foster exponential business growth.

Streamlining Processes with Automation
In the ever-evolving world of business, time is an invaluable asset. Automation emerges as the unsung hero, liberating entrepreneurs and business leaders from the shackles of mundane, repetitive tasks. The principle behind automation is simple: delegate routine operations to machines, freeing up human capital for strategic, value-driven endeavors.

Imagine a scenario where customer inquiries flood your inbox. Automation steps in, swiftly categorizing and prioritizing messages. Customized responses are generated and dispatched, sparing your team from hours of manual sorting and replying. Moreover, administrative tasks such as inventory management, invoicing, and payroll can now be handled by software, reducing errors, improving efficiency, and enhancing employee satisfaction.

Leveraging AI for Data-Driven Decision-Making
Enter the realm of artificial intelligence—a realm where machines mimic human cognition to analyze colossal amounts of data, uncover patterns, and derive actionable insights. AI algorithms process data at speeds and scales

that humans could never achieve. The implications for data-driven decision-making are profound.

For instance, in marketing, AI algorithms can analyze consumer behavior and preferences across numerous touchpoints, allowing businesses to tailor campaigns with precision. In finance, AI-powered predictive analytics can forecast market trends and optimize investment strategies. Moreover, AI enhances risk assessment by flagging anomalies and outliers, mitigating potential threats before they escalate.

Harnessing Technology for Business Growth
As businesses adapt to technological shifts, the true potential of automation and AI emerges: fostering exponential growth. The synergy between streamlined processes and data-driven insights propels businesses toward greater innovation and expansion.

Consider a manufacturing company that automates its production line. Not only does this reduce costs and human errors, but it also boosts production capacity, allowing the company to meet increased demand without proportional resource scaling. Similarly, AI-driven customer analytics enable businesses to personalize experiences, cultivate brand loyalty, and tap into previously untapped market segments.

While the potential of automation and AI is awe-inspiring, it's crucial to recognize that these technologies are tools, not replacements for human expertise. The magic truly happens when businesses find the right balance between technology and human innovation.

In the context of customer service, chatbots can efficiently handle routine inquiries, but human agents are essential for nuanced, empathetic interactions. Similarly, AI algorithms can recommend investment opportunities, but the final decision should be guided by human judgment, considering broader economic and geopolitical contexts.

The journey of integrating automation and AI into business operations is a dynamic one. Rapid technological advancements demand a proactive stance—one where businesses commit to continuous learning and adaptation.

Staying informed about the latest trends and innovations is paramount. Regular training and upskilling initiatives ensure that your workforce remains equipped to harness the full potential of these technologies. Moreover, fostering a culture of innovation encourages employees to explore novel applications of automation and AI within your unique business context.

In the realm of modern business, embracing technological advancements like automation and AI isn't a matter of choice—it's a strategic imperative. The streamlined processes, data-driven insights, and exponential growth they offer are pivotal to staying competitive in today's rapidly evolving landscape.

As you navigate the integration of these technologies, remember that while machines are powerful tools, it's the ingenuity, creativity, and adaptability of the human mind that truly steer the course of innovation. Striking the right balance between automation and human expertise is the key to unleashing the full potential of your business in the age of technology.

The Rise of NFTs and Digital Assets

The modern financial landscape is continually evolving, driven by technological innovations that reshape the way we create, manage, and invest our wealth. One of the most intriguing developments in recent times has been the meteoric rise of Non-Fungible Tokens, or NFTs, and the emergence of digital assets as a transformative force in various industries. This sub-chapter delves into the fascinating world of NFTs, providing a comprehensive understanding of their nature, exploring their potential for investment, and analyzing their potential impact on diverse sectors.

Understanding Non-Fungible Tokens (NFTs)

At its core, a non-fungible token is a digital certificate of ownership representing a unique item, work of art, collectible, or piece of content. Unlike cryptocurrencies like Bitcoin or Ethereum, which are fungible and interchangeable with one another, NFTs derive their value from their individuality and scarcity. Each NFT is stored on a blockchain, which is a decentralized digital ledger that ensures provenance, authenticity, and immutability.

NFTs have opened up new possibilities for creators and collectors alike. Artists, musicians, writers, and even gamers can tokenize their digital creations, establishing verifiable ownership and enabling them to monetize their work directly. This has led to a profound democratization of the creative industries, enabling creators to bypass traditional gatekeepers and reach a global audience.

Exploring Investment and Creation of NFTs
The investment potential of NFTs has captured the attention of not only artists but also investors seeking new opportunities. When considering investing in NFTs, several factors come into play. Rarity, historical significance, the reputation of the creator, and market demand are all key considerations. While some NFTs have commanded astronomical prices, it's important for potential investors to conduct thorough research and exercise caution, given the inherent volatility of this emerging market.

Creating NFTs involves the process of minting, whereby digital assets are tokenized and recorded on the blockchain. Creators can choose which blockchain platform to use, with Ethereum being one of the most popular choices. The minting process usually involves paying a fee and providing metadata that describes the asset. This metadata can include details about the creator, the asset's history, and any associated multimedia content.

The Potential Impact of NFTs on Various Industries

The potential applications of NFTs extend far beyond the realm of art and collectibles. Industries such as gaming, entertainment, real estate, fashion, and even education are beginning to explore the transformative power of NFTs.

In the gaming industry, NFTs enable players to own and trade in-game assets, fostering a new level of ownership and value. Virtual real estate, wearables, and unique characters can all be tokenized, creating a vibrant ecosystem where players can participate in both the virtual and economic aspects of their favorite games.

Moreover, NFTs are revolutionizing the music and entertainment sectors. Musicians can tokenize albums, offering exclusive content and experiences to token holders. Additionally, NFTs are providing new ways for content creators to monetize their work directly from their audiences, bypassing traditional distribution channels.

In real estate, NFTs have the potential to simplify property transactions by digitizing ownership and streamlining the transfer of titles. This innovation could disrupt conventional practices and make property investment more accessible.

The rise of NFTs and digital assets marks a significant shift in how we perceive ownership, value, and creativity. While the potential for investment and innovation is substantial, it's crucial to approach this emerging landscape with an informed perspective. The future of NFTs holds exciting possibilities, touching every facet of the global economy, from art and entertainment to commerce and beyond. As this digital revolution continues to unfold, it's essential to stay curious, educated, and adaptable to the evolving opportunities presented by technological advancements.

Chapter 12: Sustainable and Ethical Investments

Environmental, Social, and Governance (ESG) Investing

In a rapidly evolving global landscape, investors are seeking avenues that align with their values and principles, transcending the traditional notion of financial returns. Enter Environmental, Social, and Governance (ESG) investing, an approach that has gained significant traction in recent years due to its focus on ethical considerations, long-term sustainability, and responsible wealth creation.

Integrating Ethical Considerations into Investments

The driving force behind ESG investing lies in the recognition that businesses have a profound impact on the world beyond their balance sheets. ESG investing involves the conscious integration of environmental, social, and governance factors into investment decisions, a departure from purely profit-driven approaches. Investors now see the power of their capital in driving positive change and shaping industries towards a more sustainable future.

By integrating ethical considerations, ESG investing aims to address critical global challenges such as climate change, social inequality, and corporate governance shortcomings. This approach provides investors with an opportunity to make a tangible difference while generating financial returns.

Evaluating Companies Based on ESG Criteria
One of the cornerstones of ESG investing is the meticulous evaluation of companies based on a set of criteria that encompass environmental impact, social responsibility, and corporate governance practices. Environmental criteria delve into a company's commitment to reducing its ecological footprint, such as minimizing greenhouse gas emissions, conserving water, and adopting sustainable sourcing practices.

Social criteria extend to the treatment of employees, customers, and the communities in which companies operate. This includes factors such as labor standards, diversity and inclusion initiatives, community engagement, and human rights considerations. Meanwhile, governance criteria assess the quality of a company's leadership, executive compensation, board structure, and transparency in financial reporting.

Balancing Returns with Societal and Environmental Impact
One of the common misconceptions about ESG investing is that it sacrifices financial returns for ethical concerns. However, recent research and real-world performance data have indicated quite the opposite. Companies that excel in ESG metrics often exhibit strong risk management practices, innovation, and resilience, which can contribute to their long-term financial success.

Investors are recognizing that a company's commitment to ESG factors can be indicative of its ability to navigate challenges and seize opportunities in an ever-changing market landscape. This realization has led to the emergence of sustainable indices and funds that focus on high-performing ESG companies, attracting a growing pool of investors who are looking to create a positive impact without compromising their financial aspirations.

ESG investing represents more than just a new investment approach; it signifies a paradigm shift in how capitalism and business practices are evolving. As investors demand greater transparency and accountability, companies are compelled to not only improve their bottom lines but also contribute positively to society and the planet. This shift is influencing corporate strategies, reshaping industries, and redefining success.

ESG investing is a potent vehicle for investors to channel their financial resources towards a better world. By integrating ethical considerations, evaluating companies based on ESG criteria, and striking a harmonious balance between financial returns and societal impact, ESG investing has become a formidable force in shaping a more sustainable and inclusive global economy. As the movement gains momentum, it has the potential to reshape investment practices and inspire a new generation of conscious investors who seek to make a lasting, positive impact on both their portfolios and the world at large.

Impact Investing for Positive Change

In today's rapidly evolving financial landscape, the concept of investing has transcended mere profit generation. Increasingly, investors are aligning their financial decisions with their values, aiming to generate positive societal and environmental outcomes alongside financial returns. This ethical approach to investing is encapsulated by the burgeoning field of impact investing.

Investing in Projects with Social and Environmental Goals

Impact investing entails deploying capital with the intention of achieving measurable positive impacts on society and the environment. Unlike traditional investments solely focused on financial returns, impact investing goes a step further, aiming to address pressing global challenges such as climate change, poverty alleviation, gender inequality, and more. This approach often involves supporting projects, companies, or funds that are dedicated to social and environmental causes.

For instance, impact investors might choose to invest in renewable energy projects to accelerate the transition to cleaner energy sources. Alternatively, they might support businesses committed to fair labor practices and supply chain transparency, thereby promoting better working conditions across industries. By channeling funds into such ventures, impact investors become integral players in driving positive change on a global scale.

Measuring Impact and Tracking Progress

A hallmark of impact investing is its emphasis on measurable outcomes. Investors seek not only financial returns but also tangible evidence of the positive effects their investments are generating. This requires comprehensive metrics to gauge and quantify the social and environmental impacts of investments. Metrics can range from reduced carbon emissions to improved access to education or healthcare.

Institutional frameworks such as the United Nations' Sustainable Development Goals (SDGs) provide a common language for impact measurement. These goals encompass a wide spectrum of challenges, serving as a roadmap for aligning investments with specific societal targets. Impact investors often collaborate with organizations that specialize in impact assessment, employing methodologies that assess both qualitative and quantitative changes brought about by their investments.

Contributing to a More Sustainable Future through Investments

One of the most compelling aspects of impact investing is its potential to catalyze positive systemic change. By directing capital towards sustainable and ethical initiatives, investors play a pivotal role in influencing industries and fostering innovation. This influence extends to encouraging businesses to adopt environmentally friendly practices, promoting diversity and inclusion, and fostering sustainable business models.

Moreover, impact investing offers individuals and institutions the opportunity to bridge the gap between financial goals and the desire to create a better world. It empowers investors to become change-makers, using their financial resources strategically to support initiatives that align with their personal values. This fusion of financial acumen and ethical commitment paves the way for a more inclusive, equitable, and sustainable future.

Impact investing represents a pivotal evolution in the world of finance. It goes beyond the traditional profit-centric approach, inviting investors to take an active role in shaping a better world. By investing in projects with social and environmental goals, measuring impacts, and contributing to a more sustainable future, impact investors wield their capital as a force for positive change. As the impact investing ecosystem continues to grow and evolve, its potential to reshape the global economic landscape while addressing pressing global challenges remains profound.

Ethical Entrepreneurship and Corporate Social Responsibility

In the modern landscape of business and finance, the pursuit of profit no longer stands as the sole driving force behind enterprises. Ethical entrepreneurship and corporate social responsibility (CSR) have emerged as pivotal concepts that redefine success and inspire positive change. This sub chapter delves into the profound impact of embedding ethical practices in business operations, fostering a culture of social responsibility, and achieving financial success while making a lasting positive impact.

Embedding Ethical Practices in Business Operations
Ethical entrepreneurship entails weaving moral principles into the very fabric of business operations. This begins with aligning business strategies with values that extend beyond monetary gain. Companies that commit to ethical practices prioritize transparency, fairness, and respect across all levels. From supply chain management to product development, ethical entrepreneurs consider the ecological, societal, and human implications of their decisions.

A key facet of ethical entrepreneurship involves responsible sourcing and production. This encompasses ethical labor practices, sustainable sourcing of materials, and minimizing the ecological footprint of operations. By adhering to these practices, businesses not only contribute to a healthier planet but also build a reputation for integrity and commitment to social betterment.

Fostering a Culture of Social Responsibility
Corporate Social Responsibility (CSR) has become more than just a buzzword; it's a strategic imperative. Fostering a culture of social responsibility involves recognizing the influence a company wields and channeling it toward

addressing societal challenges. CSR extends beyond philanthropy; it involves integrating social and environmental considerations into day-to-day decision-making.

Companies embracing CSR often engage in community development initiatives, support education and healthcare, and champion diversity and inclusion. By proactively addressing societal needs, businesses forge deeper connections with consumers and stakeholders. Moreover, employees are drawn to organizations that demonstrate a commitment to a greater good, which contributes to higher morale and improved retention rates.

Achieving Financial Success while Making a Positive Impact
Contrary to conventional belief, ethical entrepreneurship and financial prosperity are not mutually exclusive. In fact, businesses with a purpose beyond profit often find that ethical practices contribute to long-term success. When companies prioritize sustainable and ethical practices, they enhance their brand image and cultivate customer loyalty. Consumers today actively seek out businesses aligned with their values, translating into increased sales and market share.

Furthermore, ethical practices can lead to operational efficiencies. Embracing environmentally friendly practices reduces waste and operational costs. A focus on employee well-being and fair compensation fosters a motivated and productive workforce. Such factors contribute to bolstering a company's bottom line while simultaneously creating a more equitable and sustainable business model.

In the pursuit of financial success, ethical entrepreneurs also recognize the potential for innovation. Addressing societal and environmental challenges can spark the development of groundbreaking products and services that address real-world problems. This not only generates revenue but also cements a company's role as a catalyst for positive change.

Ethical entrepreneurship and corporate social responsibility represent a paradigm shift in the business world, marking a departure from a purely profit-driven approach. Embedding ethical practices in business operations, fostering a culture of social responsibility, and achieving financial success while making a positive impact are intrinsically linked. As we move forward in an interconnected global society, the power of ethical entrepreneurship offers a transformative avenue for financial growth, social betterment, and a sustainable future. By embracing this approach, businesses can become champions of change and carve a path towards enduring success that resonates far beyond the boardroom.

Chapter 13: Adapting to Economic Changes

Thriving in Economic Ups and Downs

In the ever-evolving landscape of the global economy, understanding how to not only survive but thrive in economic ups and downs is a hallmark of financial wisdom. Economic cycles, characterized by alternating periods of growth and contraction, are as inevitable as they are unpredictable. However, those who possess the knowledge and strategies to navigate these cycles can emerge stronger and more resilient, regardless of the prevailing economic climate.

Strategies for Navigating Economic Cycles

The ability to anticipate and adapt to economic shifts is a skill honed by astute investors, entrepreneurs, and individuals who understand the interconnectedness of markets and industries. Navigating economic cycles involves a multifaceted approach that combines awareness, preparedness, and strategic decision-making.

1. Diversification: One of the most effective strategies in mitigating the impact of economic fluctuations is diversification. Spreading investments across various asset classes, industries, and geographic regions can help buffer the negative effects of a downturn in a particular sector. A well-diversified portfolio can provide stability during turbulent times and position investors to capture opportunities when markets rebound.

2. Risk Assessment and Management: Economic cycles are often accompanied by changes in risk profiles. Understanding how to assess and manage risks is paramount. During periods of economic expansion, the focus should be on identifying potential vulnerabilities and ensuring the sustainability of growth. In times of contraction, risk mitigation becomes essential to protect assets and preserve capital.

3. Adaptive Business Models: Entrepreneurs who build flexibility into their business models are better equipped to weather economic storms. Being able to pivot quickly, adjust product offerings, and identify new revenue streams are essential attributes of businesses that thrive regardless of economic conditions. Innovation and agility are key to staying competitive in a changing landscape.

Identifying Opportunities During Downturns
Contrary to popular belief, economic downturns are not entirely unfavorable. They also present unique opportunities for those who are prepared and vigilant. During these phases, assets may be undervalued, and new niches can emerge.

1. Value Investing: Economic downturns often lead to market undervaluation. Savvy investors adopt a value-based approach, seeking companies with solid fundamentals that are temporarily undervalued by market sentiment. By recognizing these opportunities, investors can acquire assets at a discount, positioning themselves for potential gains as markets recover.

2. Entrepreneurial Ventures: Downturns can be the breeding ground for innovative business ideas. As consumer preferences change and industries evolve, new gaps in the market arise. Entrepreneurs who identify these gaps and create solutions that address emerging needs stand to gain a competitive advantage when economic conditions improve.

3. Education and Skill Enhancement: Economic downturns can provide individuals with the time and motivation to invest in self-improvement. Acquiring new skills, pursuing advanced education, and enhancing professional qualifications can lead to increased employability and career growth, aligning individuals with higher-paying opportunities in the future.

Positioning for Growth in Prosperous Times
While navigating economic downturns is crucial, positioning oneself for growth during prosperous periods is equally important. Prosperous economic phases present unique chances to leverage momentum and optimize financial gains.

1. Capitalizing on Market Optimism: Prosperous economic conditions are often accompanied by a buoyant market sentiment. During these times, investors should consider capitalizing on growth opportunities by participating in markets and industries that demonstrate strong upward trajectories.

2. Strategic Investing: When economic indicators signal growth, strategic investments in sectors that are primed for expansion can yield substantial returns. Researching industries with favorable trends and identifying emerging technologies can allow investors to capitalize on early-stage growth.

3. Long-Term Planning: Just as economic cycles ebb and flow, so do personal financial journeys. In periods of prosperity, it's wise to engage in comprehensive long-term financial planning. This involves setting achievable goals, evaluating risk tolerance, and crafting an investment strategy that aligns with individual aspirations.

Thriving in economic ups and downs requires a blend of knowledge, adaptability, and prudent decision-making. By embracing strategies that encompass diversification, risk management, and seizing opportunities, individuals and businesses can navigate the cyclical nature of the economy with confidence. Whether the economic tide is rising or receding, those armed with the right tools and insights are better positioned to not only weather the storm but to emerge stronger on the other side.

Future-Proofing Your Career and Business

In an era of rapid technological advancements and unpredictable economic shifts, the concept of 'business as usual' is quickly becoming obsolete. As we navigate through an ever-evolving landscape, the ability to future-proof one's career and business has become not just a strategic advantage, but a necessity for long-term success. In this sub-chapter, we delve into the crucial strategies and mindset required to remain resilient and relevant in the face of economic changes.

Embracing Lifelong Learning and Skill Development

The cornerstone of future-proofing your career and business lies in your commitment to lifelong learning. In an environment where knowledge becomes outdated quicker than ever before, continuous skill development is paramount. Embracing a mindset of perpetual learning allows you to stay ahead of the curve and adapt to emerging trends. Seek out opportunities to upskill, whether through formal education, online courses, workshops, or mentorship programs. By constantly updating your skillset, you position yourself as an adaptable professional capable of taking on new challenges with confidence.

Lifelong learning isn't solely about acquiring new technical skills; it also encompasses the cultivation of soft skills such as critical thinking, creativity, adaptability, and effective communication. These skills form the bedrock of problem-solving and innovation, empowering you to navigate complexities and seize opportunities in any economic climate.

Adapting to Technological Disruptions
Technology has fundamentally reshaped industries and continues to do so at an unprecedented pace. While disruption can be unsettling, it also opens doors to novel opportunities. To future-proof your career and business, embrace technological changes rather than resist them. Engage in continuous technological literacy to comprehend the implications of emerging tools and systems.

Technological disruptions extend beyond specific industries. Even traditional businesses benefit from harnessing technology to streamline processes, enhance customer experiences, and gather valuable data for informed decision-making. Staying attuned to the latest tech trends, such as artificial intelligence, blockchain, and the Internet of Things, equips you to explore innovative ways to remain competitive.

Staying Relevant in a Rapidly Evolving Job Market
The job market of today is vastly different from that of a decade ago. Automation, remote work, and gig economy opportunities have transformed the employment landscape. To remain relevant, individuals must adopt a proactive mindset that embraces change. This means not only anticipating shifts but also honing your ability to pivot and adapt.

Networking and building relationships within your industry are essential components of staying relevant. Engaging with professional communities, attending conferences, and participating in online forums provide insights into current industry trends and potential future developments. This knowledge empowers you to tailor your skill development efforts and pivot your business strategies accordingly.

The rise of remote work and freelance opportunities underscores the importance of personal branding. An online presence that showcases your expertise, accomplishments, and insights can attract new opportunities and collaborations. It's no longer enough to excel solely within your immediate job description; you must position yourself as a thought leader who contributes to the broader discourse within your field.

Future-proofing your career and business demands a commitment to continuous learning, adaptability, and a proactive approach to technological changes. By embracing these principles, you not only safeguard your professional journey but also position yourself to thrive amid economic changes, emerging as a resilient and agile player in the ever-evolving business landscape. Remember, the only constant in today's world is change, and it's those who embrace it that will shape the future.

Crisis Management and Financial Preparedness

In the dynamic landscape of finance and business, the ability to weather economic storms and navigate through crises is paramount. While economic changes are inevitable, having a well-structured crisis management plan and financial safety net can be the difference between faltering and thriving during tumultuous times. This sub-chapter delves into the crucial aspects of crisis management and financial preparedness, equipping you with the tools to safeguard your financial well-being and emerge stronger from adversity.

Creating a Comprehensive Crisis Management Plan

A crisis management plan is akin to a strategic blueprint that outlines the steps to be taken when unexpected challenges arise. Such challenges could range from market crashes and industry disruptions to global pandemics or unforeseen regulatory changes. By creating a comprehensive crisis management plan, you establish a framework that allows for swift, effective, and organized responses in times of turmoil.

1. Risk Assessment and Identification: The first step in crafting a crisis management plan is identifying potential risks that could impact your financial stability. This entails a thorough analysis of your industry, market trends, regulatory environment, and external factors that could pose threats.

2. Scenario Planning: With potential risks identified, scenario planning comes into play. This involves envisioning different crisis scenarios and outlining appropriate responses for each. By doing so, you are better prepared to react decisively when a crisis actually unfolds.

3. Communication Strategy: Communication is key during a crisis. Developing a clear and transparent communication strategy ensures that stakeholders, including clients, investors, employees, and partners, are informed promptly and accurately about the situation.

4. Resource Allocation: Allocate resources effectively to address the crisis. This includes human resources, financial assets, and technology that will aid in minimizing the impact and enabling recovery.

5. Testing and Review: Regularly test and update your crisis management plan to ensure its effectiveness. Conduct simulated crisis scenarios and review the plan's components to identify areas for improvement.

Building a Financial Safety Net for Emergencies

A strong financial safety net is akin to a shield that protects your financial stability when uncertainties arise. It acts as a cushion that allows you to navigate through difficult times without compromising your long-term financial goals.

1. Emergency Fund: The cornerstone of financial preparedness is an emergency fund. This fund should cover several months' worth of living expenses, ensuring that you can sustain yourself and your family during periods of income disruption.

2. Diversification: Diversifying your investments across different asset classes can mitigate the impact of market volatility on your portfolio. A diverse portfolio is better positioned to weather market downturns.

3. Insurance Coverage: Adequate insurance coverage is essential. This includes health insurance, property insurance, and liability coverage. Insurance provides financial protection against unexpected medical expenses, property damage, and legal liabilities.

4. Debt Management: Minimize high-interest debts to free up resources during tough times. Prioritize paying off high-interest debts, as they can quickly drain your finances.

Learning from Past Crises and Improving Resilience
History is a valuable teacher, especially when it comes to navigating economic changes and crises. Studying past crises, both personal and global, can offer invaluable insights that inform your crisis management strategies and financial preparedness.

1. Case Studies: Analyze past economic crises and how individuals and businesses navigated through them. Case studies provide practical lessons on effective crisis response, financial recovery, and adaptation strategies.

2. Resilience-Building Techniques: Drawing from historical examples, identify resilience-building techniques that have proven effective. These could include adapting business models, finding alternative income sources, or adopting cost-cutting measures.

3. Continuous Learning: Stay informed about economic trends, market shifts, and emerging technologies. Continuously educating yourself equips you with the knowledge needed to make informed decisions and proactively respond to changes.

Embracing the inevitability of economic changes and crises is the first step towards building a solid foundation of resilience. By creating a comprehensive crisis management plan, building a financial safety net, and learning from past experiences, you position yourself not only to survive but to thrive in the face of adversity. As you embark on this journey of financial preparedness, remember that each step you take today contributes to a more secure and prosperous tomorrow.

Chapter 14: Balancing Risk and Reward

Diversification Strategies for Risk Management

In the intricate journey of wealth creation and investment, a timeless principle reigns supreme: diversification. This cornerstone strategy involves spreading investments across a spectrum of asset classes, each with its distinct risk and return profile. As we plunge into the world of diversification, we unfurl the layers of this strategy, probing its intricacies, unraveling its potential, and unraveling the snares that come with overdiversification.

Spreading Investments Across Asset Classes

Imagine your investment portfolio as a well-choreographed orchestra, each asset class an instrument with its melody, tempo, and rhythm. These asset classes encompass the entire financial spectrum, from the traditional realms of stocks and bonds to the avant-garde territories of real estate, commodities, and alternative investments like cryptocurrencies. The underpinning philosophy of diversification rests on the fact that these asset classes don't move in tandem; they dance to different tunes, driven by their unique economic drivers.

Spreading investments across these diverse asset classes insulates your portfolio from the effects of any single asset's performance. When stocks soar, bonds might be in a stable embrace, or real estate could be traversing its own cycles. This allocation creates a harmonious synergy that seeks to reduce the extreme highs and lows that can characterize financial markets.

Balancing Risk and Potential Returns

Diversification is, at its core, a tightrope act between risk and potential rewards. High-risk investments, like equities, have the potential for substantial gains but are accompanied by the unsettling specter of volatility. On the other hand, the tranquil waters of bonds offer stability but might lack the momentum for remarkable growth. Diversification melds these two seemingly disparate worlds, yielding a portfolio that capitalizes on the high-octane moments of market surges while cushioning the blows of downturns.

Yet, achieving this equilibrium is an art in itself. Asset correlation, the degree to which assets move in tandem, adds another layer of complexity. A well-diversified portfolio minimizes the impact of correlated assets by weaving together those with low correlations. This orchestration dampens the cacophony of market volatility, transforming it into a symphony of stability.

Avoiding Overdiversification and Its Pitfalls

But, as in all art forms, moderation is key. Enter the cautionary tale of overdiversification. In a zealous pursuit of minimizing risk, some investors fragment their portfolios into an array of assets so extensive that each individual investment bears minimal weight. Just as an overgrown garden stifles its flowers' bloom, an overly diversified portfolio dilutes the potential for substantial gains.

Overdiversification can lead to a loss of focus, a tangled web of complexity in managing the portfolio, and even subdued performance. The challenge is to strike a harmonious balance that provides the benefits of diversification without sacrificing the ability to manage and monitor your investments effectively. This delicate equilibrium often prompts investors to explore the world of mutual funds, exchange-traded funds (ETFs), or managed accounts – vehicles that deliver diversification without the overwhelming intricacies.

Diversification is not a mere concept; it's a symphony of strategy, a ballet of balance. By thoughtfully distributing investments across a medley of asset classes and sidestepping the pitfalls of overdiversification, investors traverse the tumultuous seas of finance with a newfound assurance. The journey to financial prosperity is paved with judicious choices, and diversification stands as a compass that has guided generations of investors toward their goals, navigating the financial landscape with sagacity and prudence.

Calculated Entrepreneurial Risks

In the dynamic landscape of business and entrepreneurship, the art of risk-taking often separates the thriving innovators from the stagnant players. At the heart of this strategy lies the concept of calculated entrepreneurial risks – a philosophy that balances the potential rewards of a venture with a thorough understanding of the associated risks. In this sub chapter, we delve into the intricacies of assessing, mitigating, and embracing risks as a catalyst for growth and innovation.

Assessing Risk-Taking in Business Ventures

Entrepreneurship is inherently linked to risk. However, not all risks are created equal. Successful entrepreneurs master the skill of evaluating risks on a spectrum, ranging from low to high impact. This entails a comprehensive analysis of factors such as market trends, competition, economic indicators, and potential legal and regulatory implications.

Diving into a venture without thorough assessment can lead to unexpected pitfalls. One must gauge the potential for market disruption, the scalability of the product or service, and the alignment of the venture with prevailing consumer needs. Additionally, understanding the financial, operational, and strategic risks inherent in the venture is paramount.

Mitigating Risks Through Market Research and Planning

One of the most effective tools in the entrepreneur's arsenal is meticulous market research. This process entails understanding customer behavior, identifying pain points, and assessing demand for the product or service. This invaluable insight serves as a compass to navigate the entrepreneurial journey.

Planning is the bridge between assessment and execution. A well-constructed business plan provides a roadmap that outlines potential obstacles and how to overcome them. It outlines the steps needed to bring the venture to life while addressing financial projections, marketing strategies, and contingency plans. By having a solid plan, entrepreneurs can make informed decisions that minimize potential risks.

Embracing Calculated Risks for Growth and Innovation
Calculated entrepreneurial risks are not about avoiding risk altogether. Instead, they involve embracing risk as a driving force for growth and innovation. Successful entrepreneurs recognize that innovation inherently involves venturing into uncharted territories. They understand that calculated risks can lead to breakthroughs that propel the business forward.

Innovation often arises from challenging the status quo and experimenting with new ideas. Whether it's introducing a disruptive product or entering a new market, calculated risks can yield invaluable insights that help refine strategies and lead to better outcomes. Moreover, calculated risks foster adaptability – a crucial trait in today's rapidly evolving business landscape.

Case Study: Airbnb's Calculated Disruption

The story of Airbnb serves as a testament to the power of calculated entrepreneurial risks. In its early days, Airbnb disrupted the hospitality industry by allowing homeowners to rent out their spaces to travelers. This was a calculated risk – the founders saw the untapped potential in the sharing economy and leveraged it to create a platform that revolutionized travel accommodations.

The founders took steps to mitigate risks by ensuring security for both hosts and guests, and they conducted thorough market research to understand user preferences. By embracing the calculated risk of disrupting an established industry, Airbnb tapped into a massive market, leading to exponential growth and a valuation that surpassed that of traditional hotel chains.

Calculated entrepreneurial risks are a testament to the spirit of innovation and growth. Entrepreneurs who master the art of assessing risks, mitigating potential pitfalls, and embracing calculated risks position themselves for success. This approach fosters a culture of adaptability, propelling businesses toward innovative solutions and growth opportunities.

In the journey of entrepreneurship, it's important to remember that not every venture will result in immediate success. However, calculated risks increase the likelihood of achieving favorable outcomes while minimizing the negative impact of potential setbacks. By leveraging these principles, entrepreneurs can navigate the complex world of business with confidence and a higher probability of achieving their goals.

Psychological Aspects of Risk-Taking

In the intricate dance of wealth creation, few elements play as vital a role as risk and reward. The allure of substantial gains is often countered by the lurking shadows of potential losses. To navigate this delicate equilibrium, one must not only grasp the mechanics of risk management but also delve into the profound realm of psychological influences on decision-making. As we explore the psychological aspects of risk-taking, we uncover the underlying biases that shape our choices, strategies to temper fear and uncertainty, and the pursuit of a balanced risk tolerance.

Understanding Behavioral Biases and Decision-Making

Human cognition, while remarkable, is often subject to systematic errors known as cognitive biases. These biases, deeply ingrained in our psychological fabric, can significantly skew our perceptions and judgments when it comes to financial decisions. Confirmation bias, for instance, compels us to seek information that aligns with our existing beliefs, leading us to overlook valuable contrary insights. Anchoring bias tethers our decisions to initial reference points, preventing us from fully considering alternatives.

Moreover, loss aversion, a potent psychological phenomenon, impels us to avoid losses more fervently than we pursue gains. This innate bias can cause us to shy away from potentially profitable opportunities out of an irrational fear of losses. Recognizing these biases is the first step to mitigating their effects. By cultivating self-awareness and consciously challenging our thought patterns, we can free ourselves from the gravitational pull of these cognitive distortions.

Managing Fear and Uncertainty in Financial Choices
Fear, a primal emotion wired into our survival mechanisms, can wield disproportionate influence over our financial decisions. The mere thought of losing hard-earned capital can trigger anxiety, often leading to hasty, emotion-driven choices. In the realm of finance, however, allowing fear to drive decisions is akin to steering blindfolded through a storm.

One effective strategy is adopting a rational decision-making framework. By methodically evaluating potential risks and rewards, we can remove the lens of emotion and replace it with an objective perspective. Building a solid understanding of the assets or ventures we're investing in can foster confidence and alleviate anxiety. Additionally, setting predefined exit points or stop-loss measures provides a safety net, curbing the instinct to hold onto investments purely out of fear.

Developing a Balanced Approach to Risk Tolerance
The art of risk-taking lies not in the absence of fear, but in the ability to manage it. Crafting a balanced approach to risk tolerance requires a blend of introspection and strategic thinking. One crucial factor to consider is individual risk appetite, which varies greatly from person to person.

Factors such as financial goals, life stage, and personal experiences shape this appetite. For instance, a young entrepreneur might be more willing to embrace risk in pursuit of rapid growth, while a retiree might prioritize wealth preservation.

Diversification stands as a cornerstone of risk mitigation. Spreading investments across a spectrum of assets can cushion the impact of losses in any one area. This approach can temper the emotional turbulence that accompanies significant fluctuations in specific markets. The essence of balance, however, emerges from understanding that risk and reward are inherently linked. Averse to rash decisions but unafraid to seize opportunities, balanced risk-takers weigh potential gains against potential losses and move forward with clarity.

The psychological underpinnings of risk-taking hold a profound influence over our financial journeys. By recognizing and addressing cognitive biases, managing fear through rational decision-making, and striking a harmonious balance between risk and reward, we can navigate the turbulent waters of wealth creation with greater confidence. In the labyrinth of finance, self-awareness and strategic acumen become our guiding lights, ensuring that our pursuit of reward remains tempered by the wisdom of calculated risk.

Chapter 15: Continual Learning and Growth In Journey of Wealth

The Role of Education in Wealth Creation

In the exhilarating journey toward building wealth, there exists an indispensable ally that can set the trajectory for success: education. Education isn't confined to the walls of academia or the structured curricula of schools and colleges. Instead, it is a lifelong commitment to learning, an unquenchable thirst for knowledge that propels individuals toward unlocking their full potential. In this subchapter, we delve deep into the crucial role of education as a catalyst for wealth creation, exploring how continuous learning can shape fortunes and transform aspirations into tangible realities.

Lifelong Learning as a Driver of Success

Lifelong learning is the cornerstone upon which the edifice of success is erected. It's the understanding that education isn't a finite period culminating with a degree; rather, it's a dynamic process that evolves alongside personal growth. Visionaries and titans of industries have long understood that the world changes at an unprecedented pace, and those who adapt swiftly through ongoing education stand at the forefront of innovation and wealth generation.

The modern landscape is characterized by rapid advancements in technology, evolving market trends, and dynamic customer preferences. To navigate this ever-shifting terrain, a commitment to continuous learning is not just beneficial—it's imperative. This philosophy encapsulates embracing new skills, staying updated with industry trends, and actively seeking out opportunities to expand one's knowledge horizons.

Pursuing Formal and Informal Education Opportunities
While formal education certainly has its merits, including providing foundational knowledge and structured learning environments, the modern wealth builder recognizes that learning extends far beyond the classroom. It encompasses a multifaceted approach that incorporates informal education opportunities as well.

Formal education often equips individuals with technical skills and a theoretical framework. However, to thrive in a competitive business world, an adept understanding of interpersonal skills, emotional intelligence, and creative problem-solving is essential. Informal education avenues such as workshops, seminars, webinars, podcasts, and online courses offer invaluable insights into these areas, allowing wealth seekers to round out their skill set.

In this digital age, information is accessible like never before. Online platforms have democratized education, enabling anyone with an internet connection to access courses from esteemed institutions and thought leaders. By leveraging these resources, wealth builders can cultivate a diverse skill set, equipping themselves to seize opportunities across a spectrum of industries.

Transforming Knowledge into Actionable Insights
Knowledge alone, while invaluable, remains inert until applied effectively. The true wealth seeker understands that education is not an end in itself but a means to an end—an instrument for transformation. The bridge between knowledge and action is built upon the foundation of critical thinking and practical application.

Every piece of information absorbed during the educational journey has the potential to become an actionable insight. This transformation occurs through a deliberate process of analysis, synthesis, and adaptation. The adept wealth creator doesn't just accumulate knowledge; they assess how it can be integrated into their personal and professional endeavors.

Education's true impact is magnified when it empowers individuals to innovate, solve problems, and pioneer new approaches. When knowledge is harnessed to create value, whether by launching a disruptive startup, optimizing investment strategies, or enhancing business operations, it becomes a driving force for wealth accumulation.

The role of education in the journey of wealth creation cannot be overstated. Lifelong learning propels individuals toward adaptability, innovation, and a comprehensive skill set that transcends formal education boundaries. The synergy between formal and informal education avenues enriches the learning experience. And, most importantly, transforming acquired knowledge into actionable insights transforms education into the powerhouse that propels wealth seekers beyond boundaries, into a realm of limitless possibilities.

Staying Updated in a Dynamic Business Landscape

In the ever-evolving world of business, where trends can shift like sand beneath your feet, the importance of staying informed about industry trends cannot be overstated. As you embark on your journey to create lasting wealth, consider your ability to navigate this dynamic landscape as a compass guiding you through uncharted waters. The key to successful navigation lies in your commitment to continuous learning, which serves as both a shield against obsolescence and a catalyst for innovation.

Importance of Staying Informed about Industry Trends

Picture your industry as a river flowing endlessly, its currents shifting with the changing tide. In this fast-paced environment, embracing a proactive stance by staying up-to-date on industry trends is your most powerful tool. As a wealth builder, your wealth is often intertwined with your industry's vitality. By understanding the direction in which the winds of change are blowing, you can anticipate shifts in demand, identify emerging opportunities, and preemptively address potential threats.

Incorporating the latest trends into your strategies allows you to position yourself as a forward-thinking authority within your field. Whether you're in finance, technology, healthcare, or any other sector, your ability to offer innovative solutions that cater to current needs can propel you to the forefront of your industry. By keeping a watchful eye on market trends, you can fine-tune your approach, ensuring your relevance and maintaining your competitive edge.

Utilizing Mentors and Thought Leaders as Resources
Imagine embarking on a treacherous journey armed only with a map drawn by those who've traveled the path before. Mentors and thought leaders are akin to this map, offering insights, guidance, and wisdom that can transform your learning curve into a strategic ascent. The value of mentorship lies not only in the advice shared but also in the mistakes and lessons learned by those who've come before you.

Mentors provide a unique perspective gained from experience, helping you sidestep pitfalls and seize opportunities that might otherwise remain obscured. Through their guidance, you can accelerate your learning, unlocking a wealth of knowledge that might otherwise take years to amass. Moreover, thought leaders—those luminaries who shape and influence your industry—offer a broader perspective, illuminating trends and paradigms that might escape your immediate view.

When you tap into the insights of mentors and thought leaders, you gain access to a network that extends far beyond your own reach. Engaging in conversations, attending seminars, and participating in industry events foster connections that can prove invaluable. In this interconnected era, learning from those who've walked the path before you is not just a smart move; it's an essential one.

Adapting Strategies Based on Changing Market Dynamics
In a dynamic business landscape, adaptability is a trait that separates the thriving from the stagnant. The art of thriving amidst change requires a willingness to pivot when necessary while remaining steadfast in your commitment to your goals. Your strategies should be built on a foundation of flexibility, able to absorb new information, adjust to evolving circumstances, and capitalize on shifting trends.

Think of your strategies as living organisms—constantly evolving to remain aligned with your objectives. Regularly reevaluate your approaches to ensure they remain relevant and effective in light of new developments. Be open to discarding what no longer serves you, even if it once brought success, in favor of methods more aligned with the current trajectory of your industry.

Adapting also means embracing a mindset of experimentation. Be willing to take calculated risks based on your newfound knowledge. Experimentation allows you to test hypotheses, gather data, and refine your strategies accordingly. It's a process that acknowledges change as an opportunity rather than a threat, enabling you to leverage market dynamics to your advantage.

The journey of wealth creation is an ever-evolving expedition, navigated by your commitment to continual learning and growth. By staying informed about industry trends, you become a strategic navigator of change. Utilizing mentors and thought leaders as resources equips you with insights that elevate your journey. Adapting strategies based on changing market dynamics ensures your relevance and resilience. Embrace this chapter of your journey with an open heart and an insatiable thirst for knowledge, and you'll find yourself better equipped to face the challenges and reap the rewards that the dynamic business landscape offers.

Integrating Lessons from Success and Failure

In the intricate tapestry of wealth creation and entrepreneurial pursuit, every thread of success and failure weaves a story of growth and knowledge. This sub chapter delves deep into the invaluable role that integrating lessons from both successes and failures plays in the dynamic journey towards financial prosperity. It's in the juxtaposition of triumph and setback that the true essence of entrepreneurial wisdom is revealed.

Extracting Insights from Both Successes and Failures
Every milestone reached, every goal accomplished, is a testament to the strategies and decisions that brought about success. These moments, while worthy of celebration, also hold rich reserves of insights. As we dissect our achievements, we uncover the specific actions, attitudes, and methodologies that contributed to our accomplishments. Whether it's the keen market analysis that led to a breakthrough product or the collaborative team dynamics that propelled a project forward, successes offer blueprints for future endeavors.

However, it's not just triumphs that offer guidance. Failures, often painted in society as setbacks, are in reality stepping stones toward growth and enlightenment. Analyzing what went wrong, rather than shying away from it, reveals invaluable data. A product launch that didn't gain traction might reveal the importance of market fit and customer engagement. A business venture that stumbled could expose the significance of thorough research and adaptable strategies.

Embracing Failure as a Stepping Stone to Growth
In the world of wealth creation, failure is not a dead end; it's a crossroads. Embracing failure is a mark of a resilient and forward-looking entrepreneur. Each misstep provides an opportunity to regroup, recalibrate, and ultimately rebound stronger. Through failures, entrepreneurs develop a robust understanding of their own limitations, identify weak links in their strategies, and cultivate the necessary resilience to navigate the challenges that lie ahead.

The shift in perspective from viewing failure as a setback to seeing it as a stepping stone to growth is profound. It transforms failure from a source of discouragement into a source of empowerment. Failure, after all, is not the opposite of success; it's a part of the journey toward success. As Thomas Edison aptly put it, "I have not failed. I've just found 10,000 ways that won't work."

Continually Refining Strategies for Improved Outcomes
The journey of wealth creation is not a static path but a constantly evolving landscape. Entrepreneurs who thrive understand that their strategies are not carved in stone but are adaptable entities. Continual refinement of strategies is not just advisable; it's essential. Integrating lessons from both successes and failures equips entrepreneurs with the tools to refine their approaches and pivot when necessary.

Each experience, whether positive or negative, contributes to the iterative process of strategy enhancement. Successes validate certain methodologies, encouraging their continuation and expansion. Failures shed light on areas that require adjustment, prompting entrepreneurs to reevaluate their approach and seek innovative solutions. It's this cycle of analysis, adjustment, and application that distinguishes a static business from a dynamic one.

The interplay between successes and failures is the heartbeat of entrepreneurship. Extracting insights from both successes and failures, embracing failure as a stepping

stone to growth, and continually refining strategies form a
trifecta of principles that drive the journey of wealth
creation forward. Entrepreneurs who adeptly navigate this
terrain not only pave the way for their personal prosperity
but also contribute to the growth and innovation of the
larger business ecosystem. The story of wealth creation is a
mosaic of experiences, each contributing a unique hue to
the canvas of success.

Chapter 16: Your Journey to Financial Freedom

Creating a Holistic Financial Plan

In the pursuit of financial freedom, a well-crafted financial plan serves as the compass that guides you through the labyrinth of wealth creation, investment, and decision-making. The process of formulating a holistic financial plan is not just about crunching numbers; it's about weaving together various strategies into a cohesive roadmap that reflects your unique circumstances, aspirations, and values. This sub chapter delves into the critical aspects of creating such a plan, encompassing the synthesis of strategies, the alignment of financial goals with life's broader ambitions, and the vital role of adaptability in maintaining the plan's relevance and effectiveness.

Synthesizing Various Strategies into a Cohesive Plan

The modern landscape of personal finance is marked by an abundance of options, from diversified investments to passive income streams and entrepreneurial pursuits. As you embark on the journey to financial freedom, the challenge lies in harmonizing these strategies into a unified plan that maximizes their potential while minimizing risks. This synthesis involves understanding how different elements interplay and contribute to your overarching goals.

Your financial plan should consider the intricate relationships between strategies. For instance, your investments might influence your tax strategy, which in turn impacts your estate planning. By strategically aligning these components, you optimize outcomes and reduce conflicts within your plan. This synthesis also allows you to take calculated steps, rather than pursuing strategies haphazardly, leading to a more streamlined and efficient path toward financial freedom.

Aligning Financial Goals with Life Aspirations
While financial goals are integral, they are only one facet of a fulfilling life. True financial freedom entails the ability to use your resources to align with your deeper life aspirations. Your financial plan should go beyond the realm of dollars and cents and delve into your aspirations, dreams, and values. It's about asking the question: What do you want to achieve with your wealth?

Whether it's funding your children's education, embarking on a passion project, or contributing to causes that resonate with you, your financial plan should be the vehicle that enables these aspirations. This alignment brings a sense of purpose to your financial journey, making it more meaningful and motivating.

The Importance of Adaptability and Continuous Refinement
In a world characterized by rapid change and evolving circumstances, the rigidity of a static financial plan can lead to missed opportunities and unaddressed challenges. This is

where adaptability becomes paramount. A holistic financial plan is not set in stone; it's a living document that should be revisited and refined over time.

Market conditions change, personal circumstances evolve, and unexpected events occur. An adaptable plan allows you to pivot, seize new opportunities, and mitigate risks. Regular reviews ensure that your financial plan remains aligned with your changing goals and circumstances. This ongoing process of refinement is not a sign of instability; rather, it's an acknowledgment of the dynamic nature of life and finance.

Creating a holistic financial plan is an essential step on your journey to financial freedom. This plan, formed by harmonizing various strategies, aligning with your life's aspirations, and embracing adaptability, serves as a roadmap toward your goals. It's a guiding light that empowers you to navigate through uncertainty and complexity, all while staying true to your personal vision of success. Remember, your journey to financial freedom is not just about reaching a destination; it's about crafting a fulfilling and purposeful life along the way.

Taking Action and Implementing Strategies

In the pursuit of financial freedom, knowledge is undoubtedly a powerful asset. Yet, knowledge alone remains dormant until it's put into action. This sub chapter delves into the critical phase of transforming concepts, plans, and strategies into tangible results. Taking action and implementing strategies is where the rubber meets the road, where dreams and aspirations materialize through deliberate steps and consistent efforts.

Overcoming Analysis Paralysis and Taking the First Steps

One of the most significant hurdles on the path to financial freedom is analysis paralysis – the state of being so overwhelmed by options, choices, and information that decision-making becomes paralyzing. While due diligence is necessary, it's important to strike a balance between information gathering and action-taking.

The first step is often the hardest, but it's also the most essential. Overcoming analysis paralysis requires recognizing that there's no perfect moment or flawless plan. Action begets clarity. By taking that initial step, you're setting the momentum in motion, allowing you to adjust course based on real-world feedback rather than hypothetical scenarios.

Begin with a simple, actionable goal. Whether it's starting a side business, investing a small sum, or setting up a budget, the act of doing propels you forward. Break the task into smaller, manageable pieces, and allocate specific time slots to work on them. Remember, progress is incremental; what matters is consistently moving in the right direction.

Maintaining Discipline and Consistency in Execution
Discipline is the cornerstone of success in any endeavor. In the context of financial freedom, discipline refers to the commitment to consistently apply the strategies and plans you've laid out. It's about sticking to the budget, consistently investing, and diligently working on your projects.

To cultivate discipline, consider establishing routines and habits that reinforce your financial goals. Automate your savings and investments, ensuring that a portion of your income is allocated toward wealth-building before you even have the chance to spend it. Set regular checkpoints to assess your progress, adjusting your course as necessary.

Mindset plays a pivotal role in maintaining discipline. Focus on the long-term benefits of your actions, even when short-term sacrifices are required. Remind yourself of the ultimate goal – the financial security and freedom you're striving for. Over time, discipline becomes a natural part of your routine, and the results will speak for themselves.

Celebrating Milestones and Acknowledging Progress
Amid the pursuit of financial freedom, it's easy to get caught up in the "end goal" and overlook the progress you've already made. Celebrating milestones, no matter how small, is crucial to maintaining motivation and a sense

of accomplishment. Each milestone is a testament to your dedication and determination.

Create a system of rewards for yourself. When you achieve a financial milestone – whether it's paying off a debt, reaching a certain level of savings, or hitting an investment target – treat yourself to something meaningful. This reinforces the positive association with your financial journey.

Moreover, remember that financial freedom isn't just about the destination – it's about the journey itself. Acknowledge the personal growth, newfound skills, and increased financial literacy you've acquired along the way. Reflect on the challenges you've overcome and the lessons you've learned. By recognizing your progress, you reinforce your commitment to your financial goals.

Taking action and implementing strategies is the linchpin that transforms aspirations into reality. Overcoming analysis paralysis, maintaining discipline, and celebrating milestones are integral components of this process. As you navigate this phase of your journey to financial freedom, remember that it's the combination of knowledge, action, and persistence that paves the way for lasting success. Your commitment to taking action is what sets you apart on the path to financial freedom – a journey that promises not only economic prosperity but also personal empowerment and a life of greater possibilities.

Embracing a Life of Abundance and Purpose

In the pursuit of financial success and the creation of passive income streams, it's essential to recognize that true wealth encompasses more than just monetary achievements. A life of abundance and purpose goes beyond the balance sheet and transcends into the realms of health, relationships, happiness, and societal impact. As we delve into this sub chapter, we will explore the profound facets of living a fulfilled life while maintaining financial freedom.

Beyond Financial Success – Cultivating a Fulfilling Life

While financial success is undoubtedly a significant accomplishment, it is merely one facet of a well-rounded and prosperous life. Cultivating a fulfilling life involves nurturing personal growth, pursuing passions, and finding joy beyond material possessions. Achieving this involves setting holistic goals that encompass various dimensions of well-being.

Imagine a life where you wake up every day with enthusiasm, driven by a sense of purpose that extends beyond your financial endeavors. This purpose could manifest as contributing to a cause you deeply care about, nurturing your creative interests, or simply making time for activities that bring you happiness. When you integrate these elements into your journey, you create a tapestry of experiences that contribute to a truly abundant life.

Balancing Wealth with Health, Relationships, and Happiness

As the saying goes, "Health is wealth." No amount of financial success can replace good health, which is the foundation for an active and meaningful life. Prioritizing physical, mental, and emotional well-being ensures that you have the vitality and energy to enjoy the fruits of your labor. Regular exercise, a balanced diet, and mindfulness practices contribute to overall wellness and can enhance your quality of life.

Moreover, nurturing meaningful relationships is paramount. Your personal and professional networks provide emotional support, insights, and opportunities that can't be measured in dollars. Sustaining these connections enriches your life and contributes to your personal growth. Balanced and healthy relationships create a strong support system that bolsters you in both prosperous and challenging times.

Happiness, often sought after but sometimes overlooked, is an essential component of an abundant life. Identifying activities that genuinely make you happy, whether it's spending time with loved ones, pursuing hobbies, or contributing to your community, can contribute to a lasting sense of contentment. Remember, financial success is most meaningful when it enhances your ability to experience moments of genuine happiness.

Using Financial Freedom to Create Positive Impact in the World

As you journey toward financial freedom, you acquire the capacity to influence the world around you positively. The wealth you accumulate becomes a tool for change, enabling you to contribute to causes and initiatives that resonate with your values. This is the essence of impact-driven philanthropy.

Consider the possibilities: supporting educational programs, funding environmental conservation efforts, or championing initiatives that address societal challenges. Your financial resources, combined with your passion and commitment, can create a ripple effect that extends far beyond your immediate sphere. It's not just about what you accumulate for yourself, but about the legacy you leave behind and the impact you have on the world.

In the pursuit of financial freedom and the creation of passive income streams, it's crucial to remember that your journey is not solely about accumulating wealth. It's about creating a life that's rich in experiences, purpose, and positive impact. Balancing financial success with well-being, relationships, and happiness leads to a fulfilling existence that transcends monetary gains. When you achieve this harmonious balance, you not only attain financial freedom but also lay the foundation for a life of true abundance and meaning.

Conclusion

As we reach the conclusion of this transformative journey through the pages of "Making Your Own Money Machine," it's time to pause and reflect on the insights gained and the path ahead. This epilogue serves as a culmination of our exploration into financial success, passive income, and the profound aspects of a life well-lived. Here, we offer a fresh perspective to inspire your ongoing endeavors and propel you toward a future of remarkable achievements.

A Journey Beyond the Pages
The culmination of this book signifies the beginning of your personal journey toward financial empowerment. The knowledge you've acquired is not merely information to be filed away; it's a guidebook for transformation. The chapters you've navigated have exposed you to strategies, mindsets, and opportunities that can reshape your financial landscape.

Remember, the essence of success lies not just in absorbing knowledge, but in taking actionable steps. As you venture forth, take a moment to internalize the lessons you've learned and envision how they will influence your decisions, actions, and outcomes. Embrace the role of the protagonist in your unique story, where you craft each chapter with intention and determination.

The Unfolding Road Ahead

Life's journey is characterized by constant evolution and growth. Similarly, your financial journey is dynamic, responding to shifting circumstances, emerging trends, and evolving priorities. Your newfound insights provide the compass to navigate this ever-changing terrain.

Consider this epilogue as a compass recalibration, inviting you to embrace the art of continuous learning. Stay attuned to new developments in finance, technology, and society. Adapt and innovate in response to changing landscapes. The pages of this book are just one chapter of a larger narrative that you will write with each choice you make.

Seeking Fulfillment in Abundance

As you embark on this unfolding journey, prioritize fulfillment as much as financial gain. The concept of abundance extends beyond financial wealth; it encompasses happiness, well-being, meaningful relationships, and a positive impact on the world. True success arises from aligning your aspirations with a purpose that resonates with your core values.

Strive to find joy in the process of growth, irrespective of outcomes. It's not about chasing happiness, but about recognizing it in every step you take toward your goals. Whether you're building a business, managing investments, or creating passive income streams, infuse each endeavor with a sense of purpose and intention.

Cultivating Resilience and Adaptability

The world of finance and business is marked by uncertainty, volatility, and unexpected shifts. The ability to navigate these challenges rests on your capacity for resilience and adaptability. Remember that setbacks are not synonymous with failure; they're stepping stones on the path to success.

When faced with adversity, approach it as an opportunity to learn, grow, and refine your strategies. Adapt to changing circumstances, pivot when necessary, and utilize your experiences as a foundation for more informed decision-making. Resilience is not only about bouncing back but also about bouncing forward with newfound wisdom.

A Legacy of Empowerment

As you progress on your journey, consider the legacy you're crafting – not only for yourself, but for future generations. Share your knowledge, experiences, and insights with those who come after you. Empower them to embrace financial literacy, entrepreneurial spirit, and responsible wealth management.

Your legacy extends beyond financial wealth; it's about the impact you've had on individuals, communities, and causes. Just as this book has sought to empower you, you have the power to inspire and guide others on their paths to financial freedom.

"Making Your Own Money Machine" isn't merely a collection of chapters; it's a catalyst for transformation. As you close this book, remember that the real journey has just begun. Approach each day with intention, embrace challenges as opportunities, and craft a life that aligns with your values and aspirations.

May your financial endeavors be marked by wisdom, growth, and a profound sense of purpose. As you step into the future, know that you possess the tools to shape your destiny, create a legacy, and embrace a life of limitless abundance.

With every decision you make, every venture you undertake, and every impact you create, may your journey be a testament to the extraordinary potential within you. Your money machine is in motion, and its echoes will resound for generations to come.